W9-DEU-761

RECIPES FROM

RECIPES FROM

THE 100TH ANNIVERSARY OF THE HOTEL UTAH
AND JOSEPH SMITH MEMORIAL BUILDING

Temple Square Hospitality

Visit us at DeseretBook.com

Library of Congress Cataloging-in-Publication Data

Recipes from the roof : the 100th anniversary of the Hotel Utah and Joseph Smith Memorial Building / Temple Square Hospitality.

p. cm.

Includes index.

ISBN 978-1-60641-934-2 (hardbound : alk. paper)

1. Cookbooks. 2. Cooking. I. Temple Square Hospitality (Firm) II. Title.

TX714.R4257 2011

641.5—dc22 2010045862

Printed in the United States of America

Quad/Graphics Commercial & Specialty

10 9 8 7 6 5 4 3 2

Contents

Often called simply "the Hotel" in the early days, the Hotel Utah was known throughout the Intermountain West for its elegance and exceptional service. Until the 1940s, the dome of the building was lit by 6,400 tungsten lights. It is now spotlighted at night. The trademark beehive which sits atop the building is the Utah state symbol and was chosen to represent the qualities of industry, perseverance, thrift, stability, and self-reliance of the early Utah settlers.

Acknowledgments

We express our deep gratitude to the following executive chefs of the Joseph Smith Memorial Building for contributing their recipes for this book: Chef Pedro Mauricio of The Roof Restaurant, Chef Scott Ackley of The Garden Restaurant, Chef Don Sanchez of the Joseph Smith Memorial Building Banquets, and Chef Val Ayrapetov of the Joseph Smith Memorial Building Bakery. Many thanks also to Megan Sorenson of Temple Square Hospitality for her compilation and organization of the recipes. We greatly appreciate the work of the Deseret Book publishing team of Jana Erickson, Leslie Stitt, Shauna Gibby, and Tonya Facemyer. Our thanks also to food stylist Maxine Bramwell and photographer Robert Casey for their beautiful work.

The Hotel Utah opened in 1911 with full hotel capability, but the Roof Gardens did not open as a restaurant until 1914. The 1911 original hotel food service staff poses here for a publicity photo.

Introduction

For the past one hundred years, the Joseph Smith Memorial Building, in all of its beauty and grandeur, has hosted millions of guests as they have celebrated the private special occasions of their lives—engagements, weddings, anniversaries, birthdays, graduations, and retirements. However, this downtown Salt Lake City landmark on the corner of Main Street and South Temple also has a unique public history.

Originally built in 1911 as a collaborative effort of local churches and businesses, the Hotel Utah was the premier hotel west of the Mississippi River. After seventy-six years as a hotel, the Hotel Utah closed in 1987. Following an extensive renovation, the building reopened in 1993 as the historic social center in downtown Salt Lake City. Gordon B. Hinckley, in the First Presidency of The Church of Jesus Christ of Latter-day Saints at that time, requested that it be renamed the Joseph Smith Memorial Building in remembrance of the Prophet Joseph Smith, the first prophet of the Church, and that it be used as a place for people to gather and celebrate important events.

The three restaurants and twelve elegant banquet rooms located in the Joseph Smith Memorial Building offer downtown dining experiences unlike any other venues. The Roof Restaurant is the signature fine-dining buffet on the tenth floor of the building, and both The Roof and the more casual Garden Restaurant, also on the tenth floor, offer magnificent views of Temple Square and downtown Salt Lake City. The Nauvoo Café, a made-to-order, cafeteria-style eatery, is situated west of the main lobby and affords ground-level views of Temple Square Plaza.

In addition to the many offices, kitchens, and bakeries needed to manage the building and the food services, the Joseph Smith Memorial Building is also home to a FamilySearch center, where patrons can research their ancestry; the Legacy Theater, where the public can view free showings of inspirational Church-produced movies; and a chapel used by members of The Church of Jesus Christ of Latter-day Saints.

We hope you delight in viewing the historic photographs as you enjoy cooking these cherished recipes from the fine-dining establishments of Temple Square Hospitality.

GUACAMOLE AND SALSA (PAGE 13)

Appetizers

6–8 servings

Shrimp with Cocktail Sauce

2 pounds shrimp, uncooked
12 cups water
2 bay leaves
2 teaspoons pickling spice
1 teaspoon salt
½ lemon wedge
1 lemon, cut in wedges, for garnish
2–3 parsley sprigs, for garnish

Cocktail Sauce

3 cups chili sauce
½ cup ketchup
1 teaspoon horseradish sauce
1 teaspoon Worcestershire sauce
1 teaspoon salt
1 teaspoon lemon juice
1 teaspoon coarse black pepper

For the shrimp: Peel, wash, and de-vein shrimp. Pour water into a large pot and add the bay leaves, pickling spice, salt, and lemon wedge. Bring to a rolling boil and add shrimp. Cook until shrimp starts to turn pink, about 6–8 minutes. Be careful not to overcook. Drain water and chill shrimp in the refrigerator.

For the sauce: Combine all ingredients in a medium bowl; mix well and chill. Leftovers may be stored in the refrigerator for a couple of weeks.

To serve, pour the sauce into a cup or bowl and place in the center of a serving platter. Arrange shrimp nicely around the cup. Garnish with lemon wedges and parsley.

Crab Cakes with Poached Eggs and Wild Mushroom Sauce

8 servings

Crab Cakes

¼ cup butter
¼ cup diced red pepper
¼ cup diced onion
¼ cup diced celery
4 teaspoons Creole spice, divided
2 cups crabmeat (fresh or canned)
2 eggs
Salt and pepper, to taste
½ cup flour
2 tablespoons vegetable oil
2 tablespoons chopped parsley

Poached Eggs

1 tablespoon white wine vinegar
1 tablespoon salt
8 eggs

Wild Mushroom Sauce

4 tablespoons butter, divided
3 cups sliced wild mushrooms (shitakes, oysters, and chanterelles)
3 tablespoons diced shallots
1 teaspoon minced garlic
½ cup vegetable stock
¼ cup heavy cream
Salt and pepper, to taste

For the crab cakes: Preheat oven to 375 degrees F. Heat butter in a small sauté pan and add diced vegetables. Season with 2 teaspoons Creole spice and cook for 2 minutes. Transfer to a small bowl. If using canned crabmeat, thoroughly drain off all excess liquid. Add crabmeat and eggs to the mixture and season with salt and pepper, to taste.

In a small bowl, season the flour with salt and pepper. Cover your hands with the flour mixture and shape patties using ¼ cup of the crab mixture for each patty. Roll each cake in flour. Heat oil in sauté pan, add crab cakes, and cook until golden brown on both sides. Transfer pan to oven to finish cooking while eggs are poached.

For the poached eggs: Add vinegar and salt to a large pot of boiling water. Reduce water to a simmer and begin stirring water clockwise. Crack eggs, one at a time, into water. They will take instant form. Cook for 3 minutes. Remove very carefully with a slotted spoon.

For the sauce: In a medium saucepan, heat 2 tablespoons of butter. Add mushrooms and shallots and sauté for 3 minutes. Add garlic and vegetable stock and bring to a boil. Add cream and boil for 3 minutes. Add remaining butter and, using a hand blender, pulse 5 times. Sauce should not be smooth. Season with salt and pepper. Set aside in a warm place.

To serve, place each poached egg on top of a crab cake and cover with Wild Mushroom Sauce. Sprinkle remaining 2 teaspoons Creole spice over the top.

Hong Kong Salmon Cakes with Baby Bok Choy

6 servings

For the salmon cakes: Heat 2 tablespoons oil in a skillet over medium heat. Add the garlic, onion, ginger, and chilies; sauté for a few minutes to release the flavor. Remove from heat to cool.

In a large mixing bowl, combine the salmon, bread crumbs, cilantro, mayonnaise, lemon juice, and egg white. Add the sautéed mixture and salt and pepper to taste. Fold the ingredients together. Form the mixture into 6 salmon cakes. Coat a nonstick skillet with 2 tablespoons oil over medium heat. Fry the salmon cakes until brown, about 4 minutes on each side.

For the bok choy and sauce: Heat and coat the skillet with 2 tablespoons oil over medium heat. Lay the ginger in the oil, add the bok choy, and pan-fry for 3 minutes to give it some color. Add the vegetable stock and steam for another 3 minutes. Remove bok choy to a plate. Add the soy sauce, oyster sauce, lemon juice, and brown sugar to the sauté pan and cook for 3 minutes until the sauce is the consistency of syrup.

Serve the salmon cakes with the bok choy and drizzle the sauce over the whole dish. Garnish with toasted sesame seeds, cilantro, and green onions.

Salmon Cakes

4 tablespoons canola oil, divided
2 garlic cloves, minced
¼ cup chopped onion
1 tablespoon grated fresh ginger (powdered may be substituted)
2 red chilies, minced
1½ pounds skinless, boneless salmon fillets, cut into small cubes
1 cup fresh bread crumbs
2 tablespoons finely chopped cilantro
2 tablespoons mayonnaise
½ lemon, juiced
1 egg white
Salt and ground pepper, to taste
Toasted sesame seeds, for garnish
Chopped cilantro leaves, for garnish
Sliced green onion, for garnish

Bok Choy and Sauce

2 tablespoons canola oil
2-inch piece fresh ginger
2 heads baby bok choy, halved lengthwise
¼ cup vegetable stock
3 tablespoons soy sauce
¼ cup oyster sauce
½ lemon, juiced
1 tablespoon brown sugar

Sweet Bay Scallops in a Phyllo Pastry with Lemon Butter Sauce

6 servings

6 sheets phyllo dough
¼ cup melted butter
24 bay scallops
1 tablespoon diced red peppers, for garnish
12 chive twigs, for garnish

Sauce

½ bottle Ariel dealcoholized Chardonnay
1 cup unsalted butter, cubed
4 ounces cream cheese
4 cups heavy cream
Cornstarch slurry
1 tablespoon Cholula hot sauce
1 tablespoon dried chives
3 tablespoons lemon juice
Salt, to taste

For the scallops in pastry: Lay out a sheet of phyllo dough and brush with melted butter. Lay another sheet of phyllo dough on top of the buttered sheet and set aside under a moistened paper towel. Repeat with the remaining phyllo until you have 3 sheets of double-stacked phyllo. Cut each sheet of phyllo into fourths. Lay 2 scallops in the middle of each square and gather the corners to form a small pouch. Pinch together so the pouches stay crimped at the top. Preheat oven to 350 degrees F. and bake on lightly greased cookie sheet for 10 minutes or until the phyllo is a golden brown color.

For the sauce: Bring Chardonnay to a boil and slowly add the butter and cream cheese and stir until well incorporated. Add the cream and return to a boil and thicken with the cornstarch slurry.* Add the Cholula, chives, and lemon juice and stir until well mixed. Adjust flavor with salt.

To serve, place 3 tablespoons of the sauce on a small salad plate and put 2 of the phyllo pouches on the sauce. Garnish with diced red peppers and chive twigs.

**Cornstarch slurry is a mixture of 1 part cornstarch to 3 parts water that is added to a boiling liquid to help thicken the sauce. Make sure to return the sauce to a boil after adding the slurry to properly thicken it and remove any starchy taste.*

Charred Pacific Salmon with Orange Marmalade and Thai Salsa

8 servings

For the salmon: Cube the salmon and then season with salt and pepper. Place a small sheet of aluminum foil on the grill and cook the salmon until it is slightly charred on one side. Be careful not to burn or blacken the salmon because it will become bitter.

For the marmalade: In a medium saucepan, sauté onion and garlic in butter until the onion is translucent. Add the mandarin oranges with 2 tablespoons of the liquid from the oranges. Add the Chardonnay and bring to a boil. Continue cooking on a medium heat until the oranges begin to break up. Add the sugar and continue to cook until reduced. If necessary you can thicken with a little bit of cornstarch slurry.* Adjust the flavor with salt, as needed.

For the salsa: Combine all ingredients and mix well, being careful not to break up or mash the salsa. Let sit for 1 hour before serving.

To serve, spoon about 2 tablespoons of the marmalade onto a small salad plate and place 2 cubes of salmon on top. Finish with 1 tablespoon of the salsa and a sprig of cilantro.

**Cornstarch slurry is a mixture of 1 part cornstarch to 3 parts water that is added to a boiling liquid to help thicken the sauce. Make sure to return the sauce to a boil after adding the slurry to properly thicken it and remove any starchy taste.*

Pacific Salmon

1 pound Pacific Salmon fillets, cut into 1-inch squares
Salt and pepper, to taste
Cilantro sprigs, for garnish

Orange Marmalade

¼ cup diced yellow onion
1 garlic clove, chopped
2 tablespoons unsalted butter
1 (11-ounce) can mandarin oranges, strained (reserve liquid)
1 cup Ariel dealcoholized Chardonnay
½ cup granulated sugar
Salt, to taste

Thai Salsa

2 tablespoons chopped fresh mint
2 tablespoons chopped fresh cilantro
¼ cup chopped yellow onion
2 oranges, segmented and diced small
1 small cucumber, peeled, seeded, and finely diced
1 small avocado, diced
2 tablespoons chopped cashews
2 tablespoons extra-virgin olive oil
Salt, to taste

6 servings

Artichoke Spinach Cheese Dip

- 6 ounces cream cheese
- 1½ cups chopped baby spinach
- 1 cup drained and chopped canned artichokes
- ¼ cup sour cream
- ¼ cup mayonnaise
- ½ cup grated Parmesan cheese
- 1 teaspoon balsamic vinegar
- ½ teaspoon red pepper flakes
- ¼ teaspoon garlic powder
- 5–6 slices pita bread, grilled

Heat the cream cheese in microwave for 1 minute or until hot and soft. Add the rest of the ingredients (except the bread) and mix well.

Cut the grilled pita bread into 8 triangles per slice.

Serve the dip hot with the sliced grilled pita bread.

6–8 servings

Deviled Eggs

- 9 hard-boiled eggs
- ½ cup mayonnaise
- 2 tablespoons Cajun seasoning
- 3 tablespoons Dijon mustard
- 2 tablespoons lemon juice
- 1 tablespoon olive oil
- 3 tablespoons granulated sugar
- 2 teaspoons salt
- Paprika, for garnish

After boiling the eggs, peel off the shell and refrigerate eggs until cool.

Halve eggs with a knife and then spoon out yolk into mixing bowl. Add mayonnaise, seasoning, mustard, lemon juice, oil, sugar, and salt. Blend together on medium speed using a hand mixer until smooth. Chill mixture for an hour in refrigerator.

Using a pastry bag and star tip, pipe mixture back into the empty egg white halves. Sprinkle paprika for garnish.

GUACAMOLE AND SALSA *(PHOTO PAGE 2)*

6 servings

For the guacamole: Cut avocados in half. Remove pit and peel. Place in a small bowl. Mash avocado with a fork or whisk until very smooth. Add lime or lemon juice, sour cream, and salt and mix well. Chill until served.

For the salsa: Combine all ingredients in a medium mixing bowl and mix well. Can be served chilled or at room temperature.

Serve with your favorite tortilla chips. To make your own tortilla chips, slice 6-inch corn tortillas into wedges and fry in canola oil 3–4 minutes or until crispy.

Guacamole

4 avocados

1 teaspoon fresh lime or lemon juice

1 tablespoon sour cream

1 teaspoon salt

Salsa *(makes 4 cups)*

4 medium tomatoes, diced

2 jalapeños, diced (use more, if desired. Remove seeds for less heat)

¼ cup diced yellow onion

2 teaspoons fresh, chopped cilantro

1 lime, juiced

2 teaspoons salt

Construction on the hotel began June 9, 1909, and the hotel was completed on June 11, 1911. Horse-drawn wagons helped dig the basement of the Hotel Utah. When construction began, it was estimated that it would cost 1.6 million dollars to build; however, the actual cost was closer to 2 million dollars.

Grilled Barbecue Potato Skins with Pulled Pork

6 servings

3 russet potatoes
4 slices bacon
2 tablespoons butter
1 clove garlic, minced
3 (2-ounce) cheese slices, cut in half
3 lettuce leaves
1 tomato, sliced
Sour cream, for garnish
2 tablespoons chives, for garnish

Pulled Pork

4 quarts vegetable stock
2–3 pounds boneless pork shoulder roast
2 tablespoons butter
1 cup finely chopped onion
1 cup finely chopped green bell pepper
2½ cups of your favorite barbecue sauce

For the potato skins: Preheat oven to 350 degrees F. Bake cleaned potatoes about 1 hour, or until a fork is easily inserted. Remove from oven and let cool enough to easily handle. Bake 4 slices of bacon on a small baking pan in the oven for 15 minutes. Cool bacon and then crumble. Set aside.

Preheat grill to medium heat. Cut potatoes in half lengthwise and spoon out the inside, leaving ½ inch of shell. You will not be using the potato that you spoon out. Melt the butter in a saucepan and add minced garlic. Brush the inside of the potatoes with garlic and butter mixture; flip over and brush the bottoms. Grill the potato skins until they are crispy, about 4 minutes on each side.

For the pulled pork: Bring vegetable stock to a boil in a large stockpot over high heat; add pork and return to a boil. Reduce heat, cover, and simmer 2½ hours or until tender. Remove pork from vegetable stock and cool slightly. Using 2 forks, shred the meat. Melt butter in a large skillet over medium heat. Sauté onion and peppers until tender, stirring frequently. Add barbecue sauce and simmer 10 minutes. Add pork to barbecue sauce mixture and cook 5 minutes to heat thoroughly, stirring occasionally.

To serve, place potato skins on a lettuce leaf. Place tomato slices on top of the skins, and then a cheese slice. Top with pulled pork. Garnish with bacon, sour cream, and chives.

Cream Cheese–Filled Strawberries

6 servings

18 strawberries
1 (8-ounce) package cream cheese, softened
½ cup granulated sugar
2 tablespoons heavy cream
½ teaspoon vanilla extract
2 oranges, peeled and segmented, for garnish

Wash strawberries and pat dry. Cut a thin slice from the stem end of the strawberries, allowing them to stand upright by themselves. At the other end of the berries, cut an X almost halfway down through the berries, creating 4 wedges in each. Set berries aside.

Place softened cream cheese in a plastic mixing bowl and add sugar, cream, and vanilla. Whisk until well blended. Place cream cheese mixture in a pastry bag with a star tip. Open up the X on the top of the strawberry enough to get the cream mixture in without breaking the strawberry. Pipe mixture into the strawberry. Garnish the serving plate with orange segments.

Fruit Kabobs and Dip

6 servings

Kabobs
8 strawberries, quartered
30 small pineapple triangles
30 red grapes
30 toothpicks

Fruit Dip
1 (6-ounce) container strawberry yogurt
7 ounces whipped topping

For the kabobs: Insert a toothpick through the middle of a strawberry quarter, pineapple triangle, and grape. Repeat process until all kabobs are made. Place kabobs on a small platter and serve with fruit dip.

For the fruit dip: In a small bowl, gently fold yogurt into whipped topping. Cover and chill.

Roast Beef and Swiss Spinach Wrap

6 servings

Cream Cheese Spread

1 ounce cream cheese, softened

2 teaspoons Cajun seasoning

¼ teaspoon salt, optional

1 teaspoon lemon juice

Wrap

1 (12-inch) spinach tortilla

2 thin slices Swiss cheese

2 thin slices roast beef

10–15 slices pepperoni

8 thin slices red onion

1 tomato, sliced

16 fresh spinach leaves

For the cream cheese spread: Mix well all ingredients in a small bowl.

For the wrap: Smooth cream cheese spread evenly over the entire tortilla. Place cheese slices at the bottom half of tortilla. Layer the roast beef, pepperoni, onion, and tomato over the cheese. Lay spinach leaves evenly over the entire tortilla. Roll the tortilla, starting from the end with the meat and cheese. Cream cheese acts as a good sealant for the wrap, or you can cover it in plastic wrap and store in the refrigerator.

To serve, slice the wrap into ¼-inch to ½-inch slices and lay the slices flat on the serving tray to show the color inside the roll. Each wrap will yeild 15 to 18 slices.

The ten-story building was considered a skyscraper in its time. The concrete and steel structure was designed by the Los Angeles architectural firm of Parkinson and Bergstrom, and the steel framework of the hotel used 3,700 tons of steel. The wings of the building were of different lengths until the renovation in 1976.

Fried Pickles

4 servings

Cooking oil
1½ cups flour, divided
1 teaspoon salt
1 teaspoon pepper
1 cup dry buttermilk pancake mix
1 teaspoon baking powder
1 tablespoon dry dill
1 teaspoon Old Bay Seasoning (available at supermarkets)
1 cup buttermilk
1 cup dill pickle juice
12 dill pickle spears

Preheat cooking oil in a small fryer to 350 degrees F. Combine ¾ cup flour, salt, and pepper in a pie tin for dredging the pickles. In a mixing bowl, whisk together ¾ cup flour, pancake mix, baking powder, dill, Old Bay Seasoning, buttermilk, and pickle juice to make a batter. Dredge the pickle spears in the seasoned flour and then dip the spears into the batter, letting the excess drip off and coating the spears completely. Gently lay the spears into the hot oil and fry until golden brown. Remove spears from the oil. Drain on a paper towel.

Serve with ranch and Thousand Island dressings. A side of carrots and celery is a nice addition.

MINESTRONE (PAGE 26)

Soups

Creamy Butternut Squash Soup

6 servings

1 medium butternut squash
2 pounds baby carrots
1 cup butter, divided
¼ cup packed brown sugar
1 teaspoon salt
1 small white onion, roughly chopped
2 cloves garlic, minced
1 rib celery, roughly chopped
4 cups heavy cream
1 teaspoon sugar, to taste†
½ teaspoon salt, to taste†
Pinch cayenne pepper, optional
Pinch ground cloves, optional
Pinch cinnamon, optional
Baked squash seeds, for garnish

†Amounts will vary depending on the flavor of the squash.

Peel and cube the butternut squash. Save the seeds for garnish. Steam the baby carrots until soft.

Preheat oven to 350 degrees F. Melt ½ cup butter. Toss the squash with the melted butter and sprinkle with the brown sugar and salt. Spread on a baking sheet. Bake the squash for 30–45 minutes or until it is soft and brown on top. The longer the squash and carrots cook, the smoother the soup will be.

In a stockpot, melt remaining ½ cup of butter and sauté onion, garlic, and celery until soft and translucent. Add the previously steamed carrots and baked squash to the stockpot. Purée the mixture well with a hand immersion blender* and slowly add cream, sugar, salt, and spices, to taste. Adjust the thickness of the soup with water to make a thinner soup or, if necessary, thicken with a cornstarch slurry.**

For the squash seed garnish: Boil seeds in salted water for 5 minutes and bake at 350 degrees F. for 10–15 minutes or until golden.

This soup is best when made just before serving. Garnish with baked squash seeds.

**In place of an immersion blender, a regular blender may be used, with caution. Be sure to vent the lid of the blender so that the steam inside does not build up pressure. Also, fill the blender only about ⅓ full so that the hot liquid does not splatter over.*

***Cornstarch slurry is a mixture of 1 part cornstarch to 3 parts water that is added to a boiling liquid to help thicken the sauce. Make sure to return the sauce to a boil after adding the slurry to properly thicken it and remove any starchy taste.*

Rough River Clam Chowder

6 servings

- ½ cup diced bacon
- 1 cup chopped celery
- 1 cup chopped carrots
- 1 cup chopped onion
- 2 cups peeled and diced potatoes
- 1 cup vegetable stock
- 3 cups heavy cream
- 1 pound chopped clams
- Salt and pepper, to taste
- ½ cup shaved green onions, for garnish
- Creole seasoning, for garnish

In a soup pot, cook the bacon until crisp; remove and reserve. Add celery, carrots, and onion to the bacon fat and simmer until tender, about 4 minutes. Add the potatoes and vegetable stock and bring to a boil. Reduce the heat so the soup is at a simmer. Add the cream and cook until the potatoes are tender, about 20 minutes. Add the clams and crumbled bacon and cook for another 3 minutes. Season with salt and pepper to taste.

To serve, garnish with shaved green onions and Creole seasoning.

Shrimp Bisque

6–8 servings

- ⅛ cup butter
- 1 teaspoon chopped garlic
- ½ cup diced yellow onion
- 1½ cups tomato purée
- 1 tablespoon Old Bay Seasoning
- 2 cups clam juice
- 4 cups heavy cream
- 1 teaspoon salt
- 2 cups cooked bay shrimp
- Salt and pepper, to taste
- 3 chopped green onions, for garnish

Melt butter in a soup pot; add garlic and onion and sauté for 3 minutes. Add tomato purée and Old Bay Seasoning; stir and cook for 3 more minutes. When it starts to bubble, add the clam juice, cream, and salt and return to a boil to heat through. Since the shrimp is already cooked, add it at the last minute. Flavor with salt and pepper, to taste.

To serve, place in serving bowl and garnish with chopped green onions.

Minestrone (photo page 20)

6–8 servings

- 1 pound ground beef
- 1 cup diced onion
- 1 teaspoon garlic
- 1 tablespoon olive oil
- 1 (29-ounce) can tomato purée
- 3 cups water
- 1 teaspoon salt
- 1 teaspoon Italian seasoning
- 1 (10-ounce) package frozen mixed vegetables (or fresh carrots, peas, zucchini)
- 1 (6-ounce) package spiral noodles, uncooked
- Pepper, to taste
- ½ cup Asiago cheese, for garnish

In a large soup pot, brown ground beef, onion, and garlic in olive oil. Add tomato purée, water, salt, and Italian seasoning. Add vegetables and noodles and continue to cook until vegetables are tender and noodles are cooked. Add pepper to taste.

To serve, garnish with Asiago cheese.

Cream of Broccoli Soup with Cheddar Cheese

6 servings

- 4 tablespoons unsalted butter
- ½ cup chopped onion
- ½ cup chopped carrots
- ½ cup chopped celery
- 2 cloves garlic, minced
- 4 cups steamed broccoli
- ¼ cup all-purpose flour
- 1 quart heavy cream
- 1 cup chicken broth
- 1½ cups grated cheddar cheese, divided
- 2 teaspoons Worcestershire sauce
- Salt and pepper, to taste
- Broccoli florets, for garnish

In a large stockpot, melt butter over medium heat. Add onion, carrots, celery, garlic, and broccoli and sauté until the vegetables are very soft. Add flour to the vegetables, making a roux. Pour in cream and chicken broth, mixing well. Simmer until mixture has thickened, about 4 minutes. Add 1 cup cheddar cheese and stir until cheese has melted into the soup. Season with Worcestershire sauce and salt and pepper.

To serve, garnish with remaining ½ cup cheddar cheese and steamed broccoli florets, divided among the bowls.

Carrot Apple Curry Soup

6 servings

- 1 tablespoon olive oil
- 12 carrots, peeled and chopped
- 1 medium onion, chopped
- ⅓ cup white wine vinegar
- 8 cups vegetable stock
- 5 apples (any kind), peeled and chopped
- 2 tablespoons ginger powder
- 1 tablespoon curry powder
- Salt and pepper, to taste
- 12 dried apple slices, for garnish
- ½ cup shredded carrots, for garnish

In a large soup pot, heat the olive oil over medium-high heat. Add the carrots and onion and cook until they are slightly brown. Once the vegetables are softened, add the vinegar and vegetable stock to deglaze the pan. Simmer the carrots and onion for 10 minutes. Add the apples and more vegetable stock if needed so that the apples, onion, and carrots are slightly submerged. Add ginger and curry powders and simmer for 45 minutes or until the vegetables and apples are very soft. Blend with an immersion blender* and adjust the seasoning with salt and pepper.

To serve, garnish with dried apple slices and shredded carrot.

**In place of an immersion blender, a regular blender may be used, with caution. Be sure to vent the lid of the blender so that the steam inside does not build up pressure. Also, fill the blender only about ⅓ full so that the hot liquid does not splatter over.*

The Roof Gardens in 1914 afforded open-air dining and spectacular, up-close views of the Salt Lake Temple and Temple Square. Glass windows were installed in later renovations to enclose the restaurant, but the roof of The Garden Restaurant is now retractable and is left open during good weather.

Avocado Gazpacho

4 servings

Slice half of 1 avocado into 8 slices and reserve on the side. Dice remaining avocado. Place in blender with cucumber, tomato, onion, broth, lime juice, and salt; blend until smooth.

To serve, spoon gazpacho into soup bowls and garnish with diced cucumber, tomato, onion, and 2 slices of reserved avocado.

- 3 fully ripened avocados, halved, pitted, peeled (reserve 8 slices for garnish)
- 2 cups peeled, seeded, and diced cucumber (reserve ½ cup for garnish)
- 1 cup diced fresh tomato (reserve ¼ cup for garnish)
- ½ cup diced yellow onion (reserve 1 tablespoon for garnish)
- 2 cups canned chicken broth
- ½ teaspoon fresh lime juice
- 1 teaspoon salt, or to taste

Potato Leek Soup

10 servings

In a medium stockpot, sauté onion and garlic with the bay leaves in butter until the onions are translucent. Add the leeks and sauté for 2–3 minutes until they begin to soften. Add the dealcoholized Chardonnay, cream, and half-and-half and stir well. Add the diced red potatoes and bring to a boil. Cover and reduce the heat to a simmer and continue to cook until the potatoes are soft. The soup will begin to thicken as the potatoes cook. When the potatoes are cooked, add the Cholula. If Cholula is not available, Tabasco may be substituted. Adjust the flavor with salt.

Serve with toasted baguettes.

- ½ medium yellow onion, diced
- 1 tablespoon minced garlic
- 2 bay leaves
- ½ cup unsalted butter
- 1½ cups sliced leeks, washed well
- 1 cup w dealcoholized Chardonnay
- 4 cups heavy cream
- 4 cups half-and-half
- 10 new red potatoes, diced
- 1 teaspoon white pepper
- 1 tablespoon Cholula, hot sauce
- Salt, to taste

6 servings

Mulligatawny

4 tablespoons unsalted butter
1 large Walla Walla onion, coarsely chopped
6 cloves garlic, finely chopped
3 tablespoons peeled and finely chopped fresh ginger
1 jalapeño, stemmed, seeded, and chopped
1 tablespoon ground coriander
1 teaspoon ground cumin
1 teaspoon ground turmeric
¼ cup all-purpose flour
8 cups chicken broth
1 cup evaporated milk
¼ cup freshly squeezed lemon juice
2 cups red lentils
2 teaspoons salt, or to taste
Black pepper, to taste
2 bunches cilantro, finely chopped, for garnish

Heat butter in a large pot over medium-high heat. Add onion, garlic, ginger, and jalapeño and cook until browned, about 12 minutes. Lower the heat to medium; add coriander, cumin, and turmeric and cook for 45 seconds. Stir in flour and cook 1 more minute. Add broth, evaporated milk, and lemon juice and bring to a boil while whisking constantly as it thickens. Add lentils to the thickened broth, lower the heat, and simmer covered. Cook until lentils are very tender, about 45 minutes. Blend with an immersion blender* for a smooth soup. Add salt and pepper to taste.

To serve, garnish with cilantro.

**In place of an immersion blender, a regular blender may be used, with caution. Be sure to vent the lid of the blender so that the steam inside does not build up pressure. Also, fill the blender only about ⅓ full so that the hot liquid does not splatter over.*

Cream of Spinach and Mushroom Soup

8 servings

2 tablespoons butter, melted
¼ cup diced yellow onion
2 cloves garlic, minced
3 cups sliced mushrooms
4 cups heavy cream
6 cups milk
½ cup water
5 tablespoons cornstarch
1 teaspoon salt
1 teaspoon ground white pepper
2 cups chopped fresh spinach

Garlic Croutons

6–8 slices bread
4 tablespoons melted butter or salad oil
2 teaspoons minced garlic
2 teaspoons Italian seasoning

For the soup: In a soup pot, melt butter and sauté onion and garlic for 3 minutes. Add mushrooms and continue cooking while stirring with a whisk until mushrooms look soft, about 4 minutes. Add cream and milk. Stir over low heat until surface bubbles.

Mix water with cornstarch to make cornstarch slurry that will thicken the soup. Add slurry, salt, white pepper, and chopped spinach to soup.

For the croutons:* Cut bread into small cubes and put into a bowl. Add butter or salad oil, garlic, and Italian seasoning. Mix well and place on baking pan. Bake at 350 degrees F. for 8–12 minutes or until golden brown.

To serve, sprinkle croutons over soup.

**Garlic herb croutons are an adequate substitute to making your own croutons.*

Civic as well as ecclesiastic leaders of the Salt Lake community were responsible for the building of the hotel. While The Church of Jesus Christ of Latter-day Saints donated the land and remained the primary stockholder, many LDS and non-LDS community and business leaders also purchased stock in order to provide Salt Lake City with a first-class hotel. The hotel restaurants and banquet rooms became the premiere locations for hosting civic and business functions. The Commercial Club poses in this 1914 photo.

Southwest Chicken Tortilla Soup

6–8 servings

- ⅛ cup melted butter
- 2 cups diced skinless, boneless chicken breasts
- 2 teaspoons minced garlic
- ⅛ cup diced yellow onion
- 2 (4-ounce) cans diced green chilies
- 2 cups tomato purée
- 1 cup frozen corn (thawed)
- 2 cups diced yellow corn tortillas
- 4 cups water
- 2 cups heavy cream
- ½ teaspoon cumin
- 2 teaspoons salt
- ½ teaspoon Cajun seasoning
- 1 diced tomato, for garnish
- 1 cup sour cream, for garnish
- 10–16 tortilla chips or 3 cups tortilla strips, for garnish

In a soup pot, melt butter and sauté raw chicken until almost cooked. Add garlic and onion, cooking for 4 minutes. Add chilies, tomato purée, corn, tortillas, water, and cream; simmer. Blend with an immersion blender* until smooth. Season with cumin, salt, and Cajun seasoning.

To serve, place in serving bowl and garnish with diced tomato, sour cream, and tortilla chips or strips.

**In place of an immersion blender, a regular blender may be used, with caution. Be sure to vent the lid of the blender so that the steam inside does not build up pressure. Also, fill the blender only about ⅓ full so that the hot liquid does not splatter over.*

Corn Chowder

6–8 servings

- ⅛ cup melted butter
- 2 tablespoons minced garlic
- ⅛ cup diced yellow onion
- 1½ cups diced ham
- ⅛ cup diced green onions
- 2 cups heavy cream
- 4 cups whole milk
- 2 cups creamy sweet corn
- 1 cup shredded cheddar cheese
- ⅛ cup water
- ⅛ cup cornstarch
- 1 teaspoon salt
- 1 teaspoon Cajun seasoning
- ¼ cup chopped cilantro, for garnish
- 1 diced tomato, for garnish

Melt butter in a soup pot. Sauté garlic, onion, ham, and green onions for 4 minutes. Add cream, milk, and corn and bring to a boil. Slowly add shredded cheese and whisk until cheese is melted. Mix water and cornstarch for thickening. Add salt, Cajun seasoning, and cornstarch slurry slowly until desired thickness is reached. Stir constantly to mix well.

To serve, place in a serving bowl and garnish with chopped cilantro and diced tomatoes.

Country-Style Chicken Noodle Soup

6 servings

½ cup diced yellow onion
1 cup diced celery
1 cup diced carrots
2 tablespoons vegetable oil
1 pound skinless, boneless chicken breast, diced
8 cups chicken broth
4 ounces egg noodles, uncooked
1 small bunch parsley, finely chopped
Pepper, to taste

In a heavy soup pot, sauté onion, celery, and carrots in oil until the onions are opaque; do not let them brown. Add diced chicken and cook until done. Add chicken broth* and bring to a boil. Add uncooked noodles. Return to a boil and cook until the noodles are done. Add parsley and pepper to taste and serve right away.

**This soup is best when made with 8 cups chicken broth. If broth is not available, you may substitute 8 cups water and 8 chicken bouillon cubes. Adjust the flavor with salt.*

Banana Bisque

6 servings

1½ cups whole milk
1½ cups heavy cream
4 bananas, sliced
¼ cup granulated sugar
1 tablespoon vanilla extract
1 teaspoon molasses
Pinch of salt

Cinnamon Sugar Croutons

¼ ciabatta loaf, cut into 1-inch cubes
3 tablespoons unsalted butter, melted
1½ teaspoons granulated sugar
1½ teaspoons cinnamon

For the bisque: Put all ingredients together in a stock pot and blend with a hand immersion blender (a blender will work as well). Chill.

For the croutons: Preheat oven to 400 degrees F. In a medium bowl, toss together bread cubes and melted butter. Stir cinnamon and sugar together until well mixed. Toss bread crumbs to coat. Arrange the bread crumbs on a baking sheet and bake until golden brown, about 8 minutes. Cool completely.

Serve bisque cold in a soup bowl and garnish with croutons.

Chilled Tropical Melon Soup

6–8 servings

1 medium cantaloupe
1 medium honeydew melon
½ medium pineapple
10–12 ounces strawberries
4 cups orange juice
1 cup piña colada mix
1 cup heavy cream
1 teaspoon vanilla extract
½ teaspoon cinnamon
1 lime, juiced
Honey, to taste, optional

Cinnamon Tortilla Chips

1 flour tortilla
Canola oil
1 teaspoon cinnamon
2 teaspoons sugar

Peel cantaloupe and honeydew melon. Peel and core pineapple. Dice all into small cubes. Cut strawberries in half.

Blend all fruits in a blender. Slowly add orange juice during blending until mixture is smooth. Add piña colada mix, cream, vanilla, cinnamon, and lime juice. If desired, sweeten with honey.

For the cinnamon tortilla chips: Slice tortilla into strips. Fry in canola oil until golden. Remove from oil and sprinkle with mixture of cinnamon and sugar.

Serve soup chilled in a small soup bowl and garnish with cinnamon tortilla chips.

Tomato Basil Bisque

6 servings

Preheat oven to 350 degrees F. Remove stems from tomatoes and place tomatoes on a baking sheet. Coat them generously with 2 tablespoons olive oil. Place in oven and bake about 10 minutes, or until the peels will come off easily. Set aside. Sauté onion, garlic, and basil in a large soup pot on medium heat in remaining 2 tablespoons olive oil. Add dealcoholized Cabernet Sauvignon and simmer about 5 minutes.

Peel the baked tomatoes and add to the pot. Purée with an immersion blender* until smooth. Add remaining ingredients to the pot and season with salt and pepper as needed. If desired, thicken with cornstarch slurry of water and cornstarch mixed together. Boil to thicken.

**In place of an immersion blender, a regular blender may be used, with caution. Be sure to vent the lid of the blender so that the steam inside does not build up pressure. Also, fill the blender only about ⅓ full so that the hot liquid does not splatter over.*

8 medium-size ripe tomatoes
3 Roma tomatoes
4 tablespoons olive oil, divided
1 medium yellow onion, diced
2 tablespoons minced garlic
1 small bunch basil, stemmed and chopped
½ bottle Ariel dealcoholized Cabernet Sauvignon (full bottles are about 25.4 ounces)
1 (16-ounce) can tomato purée
4 cups heavy cream
1 tablespoon Cholula, hot sauce
Salt and pepper, to taste
⅛ cup water
⅛ cup cornstarch

In 1912, just one year after opening, the dome of the Hotel Utah caught fire. The dome, which is twenty-two feet high and sixty feet in circumference, was not entirely consumed in this fire caused by an electrical malfunction and was quickly rebuilt.

CABBAGE APPLE SALAD (PAGE 50)

Salads

Tomato and Calamata Olive Bread Salad with Roasted Red Peppers

4–6 servings

3 red bell peppers
6 Roma tomatoes
1 cup marinated sun-dried tomatoes, bottled
1 medium red onion, peeled and julienned
1 cup calamata olives, rinsed
8 ounces fresh ciabatta bread, cubed (about ⅔ of a loaf)
1 small bunch fresh basil leaves

Vinaigrette

3 cloves roasted garlic, chopped
⅓ cup rice wine vinegar
1 cup plus 2 tablespoons extra-virgin olive oil, divided
Salt and pepper, to taste

For the salad: Roast the whole red bell peppers on a hot barbeque until the peppers are charred on all sides. Remove and place in a bowl and wrap tightly with plastic wrap until cool. Once cool, remove the plastic wrap, cut the peppers, remove the seeds, and skin and julienne the peppers.

Remove the stem from the Roma tomatoes and cut each into 8 sections. Toss the peppers, Roma and sun-dried tomatoes, onion, olives, and bread in a large salad bowl.

For the vinaigrette: Peel 3 cloves of garlic to roast. Place on a cookie sheet with 2 tablespoons olive oil (enough to cover each piece and leave some on the pan). Roast at 350 degrees F. for 12 minutes. Chop when cool.

In a medium bowl, place the roasted garlic and vinegar. Slowly add 1 cup oil while whisking well. Adjust the vinaigrette with salt and pepper to taste.

To serve, roughly tear the basil leaves. Slowly drizzle the vinaigrette over the bread and tomato salad and toss with the torn pieces of basil.

Do not dress the salad until it is ready to serve or the salad will become too soggy.

6–8 servings

Tortellini Salad

1 pound (6 cups) tortellini, cooked and cooled
3 tablespoons canola oil
½ pound fresh snow peas (uncooked), cut in half diagonally
2 cups halved cherry tomatoes
½ cup grated Asiago cheese

Vinaigrette

⅛ cup rice vinegar
1 tablespoon fresh lemon juice
1 cup plain yogurt
1 tablespoon Dijon mustard
2 teaspoons garlic powder
⅛ cup granulated sugar
⅛ cup canola oil
⅛ cup olive oil
1 tablespoon chopped fresh basil
1 tablespoon chopped parsley
4 fresh chives, chopped

For the salad: Cook tortellini according to package instructions. Do not overcook. When the tortellini has cooled, add the canola oil and mix so the tortellini does not stick together. Combine all other ingredients together. Mix and chill in refrigerator while you prepare the vinaigrette.

For the vinaigrette: In a blender, combine all ingredients and blend well. Add to salad mixture and chill until serving time.

Serve in a pasta bowl.

Marinated Mushroom Salad

8 servings

2½ pounds button mushrooms, washed
½ medium red onion, julienned

Marinade

1 cup sugar
1 tablespoon kosher salt†
1 tablespoon powdered garlic
¼ cup Italian seasoning
1 cup warm water
2 cups red wine vinegar
2 cups vegetable oil
Salt, to taste

†If kosher salt is not available, use a good quality sea salt instead of iodized table salt.

For the salad: Wash mushrooms gently and steam in a pot with ¼-inch boiling water for approximately 5 minutes or until tender. Add the steamed mushrooms while still warm to the marinade and cover with the julienned onion. Refrigerate for at least 1 hour.

For the marinade: While mushrooms are steaming, combine the ingredients for the marinade in a large bowl and mix well.

To serve, remove the mushrooms and onions from the marinade and arrange on a serving plate. Drizzle a small amount of the marinade over the mushrooms. Serve immediately.

The Crossroads Grill, which was located on the lower level of Hotel Utah, featured a live trout pond that ran down the middle of the table. It was always well taken care of, and lilies added another natural element to the trout habitat. Children were especially fond of the pond feature. In later years, the trout were replaced with goldfish.

Summer Salad with Creamy Orange Maple Dressing

4 servings

4 cups stemmed fresh spinach
2 cups stemmed and sliced fresh strawberries
½ cup feta cheese
½ cup mandarin orange sections
¼ cup candied walnuts

Creamy Orange Maple Dressing

2 cups heavy mayonnaise
¾ cup maple syrup
¾ cup balsamic vinegar
2 oranges, juiced
¼ cup grape seed oil†
Salt, to taste

†If grape seed oil is not available, use a good quality salad oil.

For the salad: Pull the large stems off the spinach and, if necessary, lightly wash the spinach leaves and pat them dry, being very careful not to bruise the leaves. Cut the stems off the strawberries and slice into ⅛-inch slices and set aside. Place 1 cup of the stemmed spinach on each salad plate and crumble 2 tablespoons feta cheese on top. Garnish with strawberries, mandarin oranges, and a few candied walnuts.

For the dressing: Using a mixer, thoroughly mix the mayonnaise and maple syrup until well blended. Add the balsamic vinegar and the juice from the oranges and mix well. Slowly add the grape seed oil until smooth and well blended. Add salt to taste. This dressing stores well in a closed container in the refrigerator up to 1 week.

Serve salad with the Creamy Orange Maple Dressing in a container on the side so that the spinach does not become wilted.

The murals on the walls of the Crossroads Grill depicted local Utah topography and were designed with a stream so that it would blend effortlessly into the live trout pond on the main dining table.

Grilled New Potato Salad with Peppers and Onions

4 servings

Preheat grill to a high heat. Slice potatoes ¼-inch thick and brush with oil. Season with salt and pepper and grill until slightly charred. In a medium mixing bowl, whisk the vinegar and mustard. Slowly whisk in the olive oil. Mix in salt and pepper, to taste. Add potatoes to the peppers, onions, parsley, and vinaigrette and toss to combine.

Serve in a pasta bowl.

- 2 pounds new potatoes
- ½ cup canola oil
- Salt and pepper, to taste
- ¼ cup white wine vinegar
- 2 tablespoons Dijon mustard
- ⅔ cup olive oil
- 2 red bell peppers, grilled, peeled, and seeded
- 2 cubano peppers, grilled, peeled, and seeded
- 2 red onions, sliced ¼-inch thick and grilled
- ½ cup roughly chopped flat-leaf parsley

Warm Italian Potato Salad

8 servings

Wash the potatoes, but do not peel. Boil or steam until tender. When cool enough to handle, peel and cut the potato into ½-inch pieces. Combine the lemon juice, olive oil, and garlic and whisk until well mixed; add the fresh dill. Season with salt and pepper to taste. Pour the dressing over the potatoes while potatoes are still warm and mix well. Serve the salad warm or at room temperature; do not chill.

- 2 pounds new red or Yukon Gold potatoes†
- 1 lemon, juiced
- 6 tablespoons extra-virgin olive oil
- 1 garlic clove, finely chopped
- 2 tablespoons chopped fresh dill
- Salt and freshly ground pepper, to taste

†A waxy potato works best for this salad. If new red or Yukon Golds are not available, regular russet potatoes may be substituted.

Sun-Dried Tomato Pasta Salad

6 servings

- 2 cups penne pasta
- ½ cup seeded and diced red bell peppers
- ½ cup seeded and diced yellow bell peppers
- ½ cup seeded and diced green bell peppers
- ¼ cup diced red onion
- ¼ cup chopped black olives
- ½ cup chopped sun-dried tomatoes in olive oil
- ¼ cup roasted pine nuts
- 1½ cups creamy poppy seed dressing (store-bought works fine)
- ¼ cup Asiago cheese, for garnish

Cook the penne pasta in a large pan of boiling water, following package directions; do not overcook. Rinse in cold running water and place into a large bowl. Add the peppers and onion to the pasta and toss well. Mix in the olives, tomatoes, pine nuts, and the dressing and lightly toss, being careful not to break up the pasta.

To serve, place salad in a serving bowl and sprinkle with the Asiago cheese.

Southwest Green Pea Salad

6–8 servings

- 4 cups thawed green peas
- 1 cup cooked bacon crumbles
- 1 cup diced ham
- 1 cup diced red onion
- 1 cup shredded or cubed cheddar cheese
- Green leaf lettuce, for garnish
- Tomato slices, for garnish

Dressing

- 1½ cups mayonnaise
- ½ cup red wine vinegar
- 1 teaspoon thyme
- ½ teaspoon cayenne pepper
- ⅛ cup granulated sugar
- Salt and pepper, to taste

For the salad: In a bowl, combine peas, bacon crumbles, ham, onion, and cheese. Mix well and chill in refrigerator.

For the dressing: Combine all ingredients in a bowl and mix well with a whisk or hand mixer. Add to the salad and chill until serving time.

To serve, garnish with green leaf lettuce and tomato slices.

6–8 servings

Cabbage Apple Salad *(photo page 38)*

4 cups chopped green cabbage
2 large red apples, cored and cut into small wedges
1 cup dried cranberries
½ cup pecans or walnuts
Green leaf lettuce, for garnish
12 orange slices, for garnish
1 teaspoon cinnamon, for garnish

Dressing

½ cup plain yogurt
½ cup mayonnaise
¼ cup rice vinegar or white vinegar
½ cup granulated sugar

For the salad: Wash cabbage and apples. Cut apples into small wedges and chop cabbage. Place in a bowl. Add cranberries and pecans or walnuts and mix all ingredients together. Chill in refrigerator.

For the dressing: In a small bowl, whisk all ingredients until smooth.

When ready to serve, toss the dressing with the cabbage mixture. Place the salad in a serving bowl and garnish with green leaf lettuce and orange slices around the edge of the bowl. Sprinkle finished salad with cinnamon.

Cranberry Apple and Pomegranate Salad

5 servings

3 Red Delicious apples
1 (12-ounce) can Sprite
Seeds from 1 large pomegranate
¼ stalk celery, diced
¼ cup grenadine syrup
¼ cup chopped walnuts, for garnish

Cranberry Sauce
¼ cup water
¼ cup sugar
1 cup fresh or frozen cranberries

For the salad: Core and dice the apples into ¼-inch pieces and soak them in Sprite for at least one hour. Peel the pomegranate and remove the seeds. It is easiest to do this by cutting the pomegranate in half and submersing it in a bowl of cold water and popping the seeds out while it is submerged. Discard the peel and pithy white interior.

Combine the apples, pomegranate seeds, and celery in a salad bowl. Toss with ⅓ cup cranberry sauce and grenadine syrup. Cover and refrigerate until ready to serve.

For the sauce: Bring water and sugar to a boil. Add cranberries. Simmer 10 minutes on medium heat until cranberries have popped and it looks like a thick, chunky sauce.

To serve, sprinkle walnuts over the salad.

The Hotel Utah hosted almost all of the banquets of early Salt Lake City. Here the lobby is utilized as a banquet hall for a prestigious formal event. Since the reputation of the hotel was so upscale, the money transacted during the day was literally "laundered." Each night, the coins were sent through a money washer so they would be clean and shiny, and the bills were exchanged at a local bank for fresh paper currency. The art glass in the ceiling today is original to the building and was covered at night during the blackouts of World War II.

Pear Salad with Walnuts and Gorgonzola

4 servings

4 handfuls salad greens, washed and dried
2 Anjou pears, washed, cored, and sliced into eighths
½ cup dried currants or raisins
2 ounces Gorgonzola cheese
1 cup candied walnuts

Dressing

2 tablespoons lemon juice
2 tablespoons rice wine vinegar
2 tablespoons balsamic vinegar
1 tablespoon raspberry syrup
¼ cup olive oil
Salt and pepper, to taste

For the salad: Divide lettuce onto 4 chilled plates and top with sliced pears and currants or raisins. Crumble the Gorgonzola cheese evenly over the 4 salads. Top with candied walnuts.

For the dressing: In a small bowl, combine lemon juice, rice vinegar, balsamic vinegar, raspberry syrup, and oil. Whisk together and season with salt and pepper.

To serve, drizzle desired amount of dressing over the 4 salads.

Oriental Chicken Salad

4 servings

4 handfuls salad greens, washed and dried
¼ cup bean sprouts
½ jicama, peeled and cut into strips
¼ cup shredded carrots
¼ cup snap peas
½ red bell pepper, cut into strips
½ cup peeled and segmented mandarin oranges
1 cup grilled and sliced chicken breast
½ cup toasted cashews
1 cup cooked angel hair pasta
20 pieces linguine pasta, fried, for garnish
1 cup fried wontons, for garnish

Sesame Ginger Dressing

½ cup olive oil
¼ cup balsamic vinegar
2 tablespoons soy sauce
2 cloves garlic, chopped
2 tablespoons honey
2 tablespoons brown sugar
2 tablespoons peeled and minced ginger
1 tablespoon sesame oil

For the salad: Divide the tossed greens among 4 bowls. Top with bean sprouts, jicama, carrots, snap peas, bell peppers, mandarin oranges, grilled chicken, cashews, and angel hair pasta.

For the fried linguine: Heat vegetable oil to 375 degrees F. Place noodles in hot oil for 15 seconds or until golden.

For the dressing: Combine all ingredients in a blender. Process until smooth.

To serve, garnish the salad with fried linguine and fried wontons. Serve with Sesame Ginger Dressing on the side.

Piña Colada Salad

6 servings

1 cup cashews
2 cups dried cranberries
1 cup diced celery
2 cups diced fresh pineapple

Piña Colada Dressing

¼ cup sugar
¾ cup piña colada drink mix
1½ cups sour cream

For the salad: Place cashews, cranberries, celery, and pineapple in a mixing bowl. Fold Piña Colada Dressing over salad mixture until each piece is evenly coated. Serve immediately or store in an airtight container in the refrigerator.

For the dressing: In a separate bowl, whisk together sugar, drink mix, and sour cream until well blended.

Serve in a medium serving bowl.

Papaya and Feta Salad

4 servings

1 large papaya, seeded and diced (about 3 cups)
½ cup chopped fresh mint leaves
3 tablespoons extra-virgin olive oil
1 tablespoon lime juice
¼ cup honey
Salt and pepper, to taste
1 cup crumbled feta cheese, for garnish

Place the papaya and mint leaves in a medium bowl. In a separate bowl, whisk together the oil, lime juice, and honey. Drizzle the dressing over the papaya and mint leaves, season with salt and pepper, and toss to coat.

To serve, divide the salad among 4 plates and sprinkle with crumbled feta cheese.

Raspberry Chicken Salad

4 servings

4 handfuls salad greens, washed and dried
1 cup fresh raspberries
1 cup medium-diced Fuji apples
⅛ cup finely diced sweet red onion
½ cup crumbled feta cheese
1 cup candied walnuts
1 cup grilled and sliced chicken breast

Raspberry Vinaigrette
1 cup fresh raspberries
¼ cup apple cider vinegar
2 teaspoons sugar
1 tablespoon Dijon mustard
¼ cup olive oil

For the salad: Prepare the vinaigrette and place in the bottom of a chilled bowl. Add salad greens and toss. Divide the tossed greens among 4 plates. Top with raspberries, apples, onion, cheese, walnuts, and chicken.

For the vinaigrette: Combine all of the ingredients, except olive oil, in a food processor. Purée until smooth. Slowly add oil until emulsified.

BARBECUED BRISKET WITH HUCKLEBERRY BARBECUE SAUCE (PAGE 74)

Entrées

6–8 servings

Baked Chicken Cordon Bleu

6 skinless, boneless chicken breasts
12 thin slices of ham
12 slices Swiss cheese
1 cup all-purpose flour
3 eggs, beaten
2 cups bread crumbs
6 tablespoons butter, melted

Alfredo Sauce

2 teaspoons melted butter
1 tablespoon diced onion
½ teaspoon chopped garlic
1 cup heavy cream
1 cup whole milk
½ cup grated Parmesan cheese
½ teaspoon salt
¼ teaspoon white pepper

For the chicken cordon bleu: Pound each chicken breast with a meat mallet to about ¼-inch thick. Place 2 slices of ham and 2 slices of Swiss cheese on each flattened chicken breast and roll it up jelly roll style. Freeze rolled breasts until completely frozen.

Place the flour, eggs, and bread crumbs in three separate shallow containers.

Dredge the frozen chicken breast in the flour; next dip it into the eggs; and finally coat it in the bread crumbs. Make sure the entire chicken breast roll is covered evenly. Freeze again.

When ready to bake, brush melted butter on the frozen rolled chicken and bake at 350 degrees F. until the meat thermometer registers 165 degrees F. internally, about 30–45 minutes.

For the Alfredo sauce: In a small saucepan, melt butter and sauté onion and garlic for 3 minutes. Add cream and milk. Stir with a whisk and slowly add Parmesan cheese once the cream and milk begin to bubble. Keep stirring until cheese is melted. Add salt and white pepper. Makes 2 cups.

To serve, cut chicken roll into wheels for presentation and spoon Alfredo sauce on top.

Chicken Alfredo

6 servings

3 skinless, boneless chicken breasts
1 teaspoon crushed garlic
2 tablespoons extra-virgin olive oil, divided
2 cups heavy cream
8 ounces grated Asiago cheese
1 (10-ounce) package fettuccine, cooked
1 tablespoon unsalted butter
½ red bell pepper
½ green bell pepper
½ yellow bell pepper
¼ small red onion
½ cup broccoli florets
½ cup baby carrots
Salt and pepper, to taste
2 teaspoons chopped fresh thyme, for garnish

Dice the chicken into ½-inch cubes and sauté with the garlic in 1 tablespoon oil. Add the cream and bring to a boil. Stir in the Asiago cheese and let the sauce reduce until thickened. Add the pasta and toss until it is well coated. Set aside.

Slice the peppers and onion and sauté with the remaining tablespoon oil and the butter. Add the broccoli florets and carrots to the peppers and onion and continue to sauté until all is heated through. Do not let it brown.

To serve, place the pasta and chicken onto a serving plate. Spoon the vegetables onto the chicken and pasta mixture. Season with salt and pepper and garnish with fresh thyme. Serve immediately.

One section of the interior seating of the Roof Gardens was focused around small booths. This booth seating arrangement is still one of the distinct attractions of the current Roof Restaurant buffet.

Chesapeake Chicken with Saffron Cream Sauce

5 servings

For the chicken: Sauté the ham, mushrooms, peppers, and garlic in butter until the mushrooms begin to brown. Add the spinach and cook until the spinach begins to wilt. Add the juice and vinegar and mix well. Add the bread cubes and cream, making sure that everything is mixed evenly. Remove the pan from the stove, sprinkle mixture with cayenne pepper and salt, and pour in the egg yolks, mixing well. Do not cook the stuffing any further after adding the yolks.

Butterfly cut the flat side of the chicken breast, creating a pocket (see page 71 for instructions on butterfly cutting a chicken), and put 2 tablespoons of the stuffing in each breast. Roll up tightly. Pin the edges with a toothpick. Sauté in a hot pan with oil until browned and place on a greased baking sheet. Bake in a 350 degree F. oven until an internal temperature of 165 degrees F. is reached, approximately 15–18 minutes.

For the sauce: Sauté the onion and garlic in butter and saffron until translucent; do not let them get brown. Add the mushrooms and sauté until they begin to soften. Add the cream and dealcoholized Chardonnay and bring to a boil. Reduce to a simmer and cook uncovered for 10 minutes, stirring constantly. Add the chicken base and adjust the flavor with salt. If necessary, thicken the sauce with a little cornstarch slurry.*

This is best served with sautéed spinach and egg noodles. For the best presentation, cover only half of the chicken and noodles with the sauce so that the stuffing is visible.

**Cornstarch slurry is a mixture of 1 part cornstarch to 3 parts water that is added to a boiling liquid to help thicken the sauce. Make sure to return the sauce to a boil after adding the slurry to properly thicken it and remove any starchy taste.*

¼ cup diced cooked ham
¾ cup diced button mushrooms
¼ cup diced red pepper
1 tablespoon crushed garlic
2 tablespoons butter
2 cups stemmed and chopped spinach
3 tablespoons pear or apricot juice
3 tablespoons rice wine vinegar
1½ cups cubed white bread
⅓ cup heavy cream
1 teaspoon cayenne pepper
1 teaspoon kosher salt
2 egg yolks
5 (6-ounce) chicken breasts, skinless, boneless
2 tablespoons olive oil

Saffron Cream Sauce

¼ cup diced yellow onion
1 clove garlic, chopped
2 tablespoons butter
1 pinch saffron
½ cup diced button mushrooms
1 cup heavy cream
1 cup Ariel dealcoholized Chardonnay
2 teaspoons chicken base†
Salt, to taste

†Chicken base is preferred because it has a fuller chicken flavor and less salt, but 2 chicken bouillon cubes may be substituted.

Serves 6–8

Chicken and Asparagus Crêpes

Crêpes

4 eggs
1 cup flour
1 cup milk
1 teaspoon salt
2 tablespoons sugar

Filling

2 tablespoons butter
16 ounces condensed cream of mushroom soup
½ small onion, chopped
⅛ cup Worcestershire sauce
¼ cup shredded Fontina cheese
1 cup chopped cooked chicken
36 asparagus spears, steamed until tender

Topping

½ cup shredded Swiss cheese
½ cup diced red peppers, for garnish

For the crêpes: Beat all ingredients until smooth. Spray an 8 or 10-inch skillet with cooking spray and heat to medium heat. Pour about ⅓ cup batter into the skillet, tilting it so the batter moves quickly to cover the bottom of the skillet. Cook until the edges start to curl. Carefully flip to the other side and cook for another minute. Continue the process until the batter is gone. You may need to coat the bottom of the skillet with cooking spray every few crêpes.

Preheat oven to 350 degrees F. Lightly grease a 9 x 13-inch baking pan.

For the filling: In a large skillet, melt butter over medium heat. Add cream of mushroom soup and onion and cook for 2 minutes. Stir in Worcestershire sauce, Fontina cheese, and chicken. Cook until cheese is melted.

To assemble crêpes, spoon ¼ cup of chicken mixture down the center third of each crêpe. Place 3 asparagus spears over the chicken mixture. Fold edges of the crêpe over the filling. Place, seam side up, in prepared baking dish. Sprinkle ½ cup Swiss cheese over crêpes. Bake for 10 minutes, until cheese is melted and crêpes are heated through.

Garnish with remaining sauce from the filling and sprinkle with diced red peppers.

4 servings

Artichoke-Stuffed Chicken

Stuffing

1 (6-ounce) jar artichoke hearts, drained and chopped
¼ cup crumbled feta cheese
¼ cup blue cheese crumbles
¼ cup grated Parmesan cheese
1 twig thyme, finely chopped

Chicken

4 skinless, boneless chicken breasts
½ cup whole milk
3 eggs
½ cup flour
2 cups fine bread crumbs

Sauce

½ cup unsalted butter
¼ cup diced onion
1 (6-ounce) jar artichoke hearts, drained and chopped
1 bay leaf
1 teaspoon dry thyme
1 cup heavy cream
3 tablespoons Parmesan cheese
3 tablespoons blue cheese crumbles

For the stuffing: Combine all the ingredients for the stuffing in a bowl. Mix well and set aside.

For the chicken: Butterfly-cut the chicken breasts to create a small pocket for the stuffing (see page 71 for instructions on butterfly cutting a chicken). Pat each chicken breast dry and cover with 2 tablespoons of the artichoke stuffing. Roll the breasts so that all the stuffing stays inside the rolls. Mix the milk with the eggs and whisk until the eggs are mixed in well. Dredge the chicken rolls in the flour, dust off the excess flour, and then dip into the egg and milk mixture. Roll in the bread crumbs, coating well. Bake on a greased baking sheet at 350 degrees F. until an internal temperature of 165 degrees F. is reached, about 15–20 minutes.

For the sauce: In a medium saucepan, melt the butter and sauté the onion until translucent; do not let brown. Add the artichoke hearts, bay leaf, thyme, and cream and bring to a boil. Slowly add the cheeses and return to a boil, making sure that the cheese is all melted.

To serve, place one piece of chicken on each plate and cover with sauce, drizzling some sauce onto the plate. This dish is best served with a hearty potato.

Coq au Vin

8 servings

6 strips bacon, cut into 1-inch pieces
2 (3½-pound) chickens, each cut into 8 pieces, skin removed
½ cup flour
2 tablespoons olive oil
12 garlic cloves, chopped
1 medium onion, finely chopped
3 carrots, halved lengthwise and cut into 1-inch lengths
1 cup Ariel dealcoholized Cabernet Sauvignon
1½ cups chicken stock or broth
¾ cup chopped canned whole tomatoes (reserve juice)
½ teaspoon chopped fresh thyme
½ teaspoon salt
1 tablespoon chopped parsley, for garnish

In a large braising pan or flameproof casserole, cook the cut bacon over medium-high heat for about 5 minutes, or until crisp. With a slotted spoon, transfer bacon to paper towels to drain. Dredge chicken in flour, shaking off excess. Add oil to a large saucepan and heat over medium heat. Add chicken and sauté about 4 minutes per side, or until golden brown. Transfer chicken to a plate.

Add garlic and onion to pan and cook for about 5 minutes, or until onion is lightly golden. Add carrots and cook about 5 minutes, or until lightly colored. Add dealcoholized Cabernet Sauvignon and cook 5 minutes or until reduced by half. Add broth, tomatoes with their juice, thyme, and salt and bring to a boil. Return chicken and bacon to pan and bring to a boil. Reduce heat to low, cover and simmer chicken about 20 minutes, turning pieces midway or when breast meat is tender. Remove breasts and set aside. Continue cooking the rest of chicken about 15 minutes more, or until tender. Return breast meat to pan and cook for about 2 minutes or until warmed through.

To serve, transfer chicken to a serving platter, if desired, and garnish with chopped parsley. This is best served with oven-roasted new red potatoes.

Lobster-Stuffed Chicken

6 servings

6 chicken breasts
1 garlic clove, minced
½ medium yellow onion, diced
1 teaspoon thyme
1 tablespoon butter
1 cup lump lobster meat†
¼ teaspoon cayenne pepper
1 cup cubed day-old bread
½ cup heavy cream
¼ cup rice wine vinegar
1 egg, beaten
2 tablespoons olive oil

†Available in the frozen section of most supermarkets.

Sauce Americaine

1 tablespoon unsalted butter
1 medium yellow onion, chopped
1 small clove garlic
½ teaspoon dried tarragon leaves
½ teaspoon dried thyme
1 teaspoon paprika
1 (8-ounce) can chopped tomatoes, drained
2 tablespoons tomato paste
1 cup heavy cream
1 tablespoon lobster base†
1 tablespoon cornstarch
2 tablespoons water

†Available in supermarkets near the bouillon.

For the chicken: To butterfly cut the chicken, press the chicken breast firmly against the cutting board with your nondominant hand. Cut the breast almost in half horizontally, leaving it connected by about ½ inch along the center length. Open it up like a book.

In a medium skillet, sauté the garlic, onion, and thyme in butter on low heat until the onion is translucent. Do not let the garlic burn. Add the lobster meat and the cayenne pepper and continue cooking for 2–3 minutes. Add the bread cubes and mix well with the lobster and onion. Slowly mix in the cream and vinegar until well incorporated. Add the beaten egg to the stuffing mixture and remove from heat.

Place approximately 2 tablespoons of the stuffing into each chicken breast and roll the breast up and pin with a toothpick. Sauté the stuffed breasts in a hot sauté pan with olive oil until golden and place onto a greased baking sheet. Finish cooking in a 350 degree F. oven until an internal temperature of 165 degrees is reached, about 20–30 minutes.

For the sauce: Heat a medium saucepan on medium heat to melt the butter and sauté the onion, garlic, herbs, and paprika for about 5 minutes. Add the tomatoes and tomato paste and simmer, stirring, for 5 minutes. Add the cream and lobster base and return to a boil. While waiting for the sauce to boil, mix the cornstarch into 2 tablespoons of water and set aside. When the sauce boils, slowly add the cornstarch slurry into the sauce, stirring constantly until the sauce begins to thicken. Remove from heat and serve immediately.

While still warm, slice the chicken pieces and arrange on a plate with buttered egg noodles and sautéed spinach. Drizzle Sauce Americaine over the top.

6 servings

Crusted Sesame Chicken with Orange Ginger Sauce

6 (5-ounce) boneless chicken breasts
1½ cups sesame seeds
1 teaspoon salt
2 tablespoons canola oil

Orange Ginger Sauce

1 tablespoon canola oil
1 teaspoon peeled and finely chopped ginger root
1 teaspoon minced garlic
2 cups orange marmalade
½ cup orange juice or water
2 teaspoons brown sugar
½ cup soy sauce

For the chicken: Thaw chicken, if frozen. Dip or sprinkle sesame seeds on the skin side only and season with salt.

Pour the oil into a skillet and heat to 350 degrees F. Place chicken in the heated skillet and sauté until light golden brown. Place chicken on a baking pan and finish baking in a 350 degree F. oven, or until the thermometer registers an internal temperature of 165 degrees F.

For the sauce: In a saucepan, heat the oil and add the ginger root and garlic. Sauté for three minutes. Add the marmalade, orange juice or water, brown sugar, and soy sauce and stir on low heat until the mixture bubbles. If you prefer a thicker sauce, thicken with cornstarch slurry.* Remove from the heat and serve over chicken.

Chicken and sauce are best served with rice.

**Cornstarch slurry is a mixture of 1 part cornstarch to 3 parts water that is added to a boiling liquid to help thicken the sauce. Make sure to return the sauce to a boil after adding the slurry to properly thicken it and remove any starchy taste.*

Barbecued Brisket with Huckleberry Barbecue Sauce (photo page 60)

8 servings

- 1 (6-pound) beef brisket, trimmed
- 1 teaspoon chopped garlic
- ½ teaspoon freshly ground black pepper
- ½ teaspoon kosher salt
- 1 tablespoon olive oil
- 2 large onions, chopped into large pieces
- 3 carrots, halved
- 1 stalk celery, cut into 5-inch pieces
- 2 bay leaves
- 4 cups hot vegetable stock

Huckleberry Barbecue Sauce

- 1 (14.5-ounce) can diced tomatoes with juice
- ½ (6-ounce) can tomato paste
- 1 tablespoon apple cider vinegar
- 1 teaspoon balsamic vinegar
- 2 teaspoons Worcestershire sauce
- ½ cup brown sugar
- 1 teaspoon molasses
- 1 tablespoon huckleberry jam
- 1 teaspoon liquid smoke
- 1 teaspoon onion powder
- 1 teaspoon yellow mustard
- 1 teaspoon minced garlic
- 1 teaspoon freshly ground black pepper
- 1 teaspoon kosher salt

For the brisket: Rub brisket with garlic, pepper, and salt. Drizzle the oil over the brisket and rub into the meat. Heat barbecue grill to a medium temperature. Place the brisket on the hot rack and sear well on both sides. Smoke the brisket by placing hot coals on the right side of the grill and the brisket on the left. Next, place hickory-smoked wood chips in a tin pan over the coals and shut the lid. Keep the wood chips smoldering. If they catch on fire, sprinkle them with water. Smoke for 1 hour.

Make a bed of onions, carrots, and celery in a roasting pan and then place the brisket fat side up on the bed of vegetables. Add the bay leaves. Pour enough stock in the pan to cover the bottom 1 to 1½ inches. Cover and roast for 4½ hours in a 350 degree F. oven. Remove from the oven, cover, and let sit for 1 hour before slicing.

For the sauce: In a medium saucepan, bring the tomatoes, tomato paste, cider vinegar, balsamic vinegar, and Worcestershire sauce to a boil. Reduce heat and simmer for 10 minutes. Add the rest of the ingredients and bring back to a boil. Reduce the heat and simmer for another 10 minutes. Allow the sauce to cool. Purée the sauce in a blender until smooth.

To serve, drizzle warm sauce over the vegetables and sliced brisket.

Marinated Sirloin Steak

6–8 servings

3 pounds sirloin steak
2 parsley sprigs, for garnish

Marinade

1 cup soy sauce
1 cup pineapple juice
¼ cup canola oil
2 cloves garlic, minced
2 teaspoons brown sugar
1 teaspoon ground ginger

For the steaks: Cut steaks into eight 6-ounce portions and place in a shallow baking dish. Pour marinade over steaks, distributing evenly over the meat. Cover and refrigerate for 6 to 24 hours.

For the marinade: Stir together soy sauce, pineapple juice, oil, garlic, brown sugar, and ginger. Set aside.

After marinating, remove steaks from the baking pan. Drain and then place steaks on a broiler pan in the oven or on the grill. For medium-rare, turn once during an 8–10-minute period.

To serve, slice the meat diagonally across the grain into very thin slices and place on a serving platter. Garnish the plate with parsley sprigs.

Downtown Salt Lake City and, in particular, the area surrounding Temple Square Plaza, has long been a tourist attraction. This 1914 sightseeing bus was a harbinger of things to come. By 2010, over 5 million people were visiting Temple Square Plaza each year. The white-glazed terra cotta and brick Hotel Utah is in the background.

Tournedos of Beef

6 servings

- 12 slices beef tenderloin, 2-inches thick or 2-ounce portions
- 1 teaspoon salt
- 1 teaspoon coarse black pepper
- 1 tablespoon butter

Sauce

- Pan juices from baking pan
- ¼ cup flour
- ½ cup butter
- 1 cup water
- 1 teaspoon beef base
- 1 teaspoon lemon juice
- ¼ cup chopped parsley

For the tenderloin: Season both sides of the tenderloin slices with salt and pepper. In a heavy skillet, melt the butter and brown the meat quickly on both sides. Remove meat from skillet and place onto a baking pan and finish cooking in the oven at 325 degrees F. for 5–10 minutes. For medium-rare, cook until meat thermometer registers an internal temperature of 140 degrees F.

For the sauce: Using a whisk, combine the pan juices with flour and butter and stir constantly over low heat for 2 minutes. Add water, beef base, lemon juice, and parsley and simmer for 5 minutes or until sauce thickens.

To serve, spoon the sauce over the beef.

Meat Loaf

6–8 servings

- 3 pounds ground beef
- 1 cup diced yellow onion
- 3 eggs, beaten
- 1 cup bread crumbs
- 1 teaspoon red pepper
- ¼ teaspoon cayenne pepper
- 1 cup tomato purée
- 1 cup ketchup
- 1 teaspoon salt

Sauce

- 2 cups tomato sauce
- 2 cups water
- 2 teaspoons white wine vinegar
- 2 teaspoons Dijon mustard
- 1 tablespoon brown sugar

For the meat loaf: Combine all ingredients in a large bowl and mix well. Mold into a loaf shape and place into a large loaf pan. Cover with aluminum foil and bake at 350 degrees F. for 1½ hours.

For the sauce: Combine all ingredients and mix well. After meatloaf has been baking 45 minutes, brush half of the sauce over the partially cooked meat loaf and continue baking. Set remaining sauce aside in a saucepan and bring to a boil right before serving.

Spoon hot sauce over completely cooked meat loaf prior to serving.

Flank Steak with Sour Cream and Mushrooms

6–8 servings

3 pounds flank steak
½ cup all-purpose flour
1 teaspoon salt
½ teaspoon white pepper
2 tablespoons butter

Sauce
1 tablespoon flour
2 tablespoons butter
2 cups sliced mushrooms
1 cup water
2 tablespoons sour cream
2 tablespoons Dijon mustard
1 teaspoon salt
½ teaspoon ground white pepper

For the steak: Mix flour, salt, and pepper in a medium bowl. Coat the meat with the mixture on both sides. Melt the butter in a large skillet and quickly brown the meat on both sides. Reserve meat juices. Place steak in a baking pan or tray and bake in the oven at 325 degrees F. until the meat reaches an internal temperature of 140 degrees F., about 20–30 minutes, depending on how well done you like the meat.

For the sauce: Combine flour and butter in a warm skillet and whisk together. Pour the remaining juices from the meat pan into the butter and flour mixture and continue whisking. Add mushrooms and simmer for 3 minutes. Add water, sour cream, mustard, salt, and pepper. Mix well. Simmer 5 minutes.

To serve, spoon sauce over thinly sliced flank steak.

From its earliest days, the open-air restaurant on the tenth floor has provided breathtaking views of the Salt Lake Valley through its southern exposure. During its full tenure, the restaurant has been known as the Roof Gardens, the Starlite Gardens, the Sky Room, and currently The Garden Restaurant and The Roof Restaurant. As the Starlite Gardens, it not only offered excellent food, but great dance music and a romantic atmosphere.

Rolled Flank Steak

6–8 servings

Stuffing

1 (10-ounce) package frozen chopped spinach
1 egg, beaten
1 cup herb-seasoned stuffing mix
½ teaspoon onion powder
¼ teaspoon black pepper

Steak

3 pounds flank steak
1 (8-ounce) can tomato sauce with onions
1¼ cups water, divided
2 teaspoons cornstarch

For the stuffing: Thaw and drain spinach, pressing out all excess moisture. Combine spinach with beaten egg in a bowl. Stir in seasoned stuffing mix, onion powder, and pepper. Mix well and set aside.

For the steak: With a meat mallet, pound out the flank steak to about ¼-inch thick. Spread stuffing on top of the steak and roll the steak jelly roll style. Secure roll with a string. Place the steak roll in a baking pan and set aside.

In a separate bowl, stir together tomato sauce and 1 cup water and pour over the steak roll. Cover baking pan and bake in a 325 degree F. oven for 1 hour or until meat thermometer registers an internal temperature of 140 degrees F. (for medium-rare). In a saucepan, stir together ¼ cup water and cornstarch with juices from the baking pan. Stir continually over low heat until it is thickened and bubbly.

To serve, transfer the steak roll to a serving platter and remove strings. Slice steak roll to desired portion sizes. Top with the sauce from the pan or serve sauce on the side.

6 servings

VEGETARIAN LASAGNA *(PHOTO PAGE 122)*

1 cup roughly chopped artichoke hearts
1 cup sun-dried tomatoes, marinated in olive oil,† drained, divided
½ medium onion, diced
2 tablespoons olive oil
4 cups roughly chopped spinach
1 cup sliced mushrooms, divided
4 cups marinara sauce,‡ divided
1 (16-ounce) package lasagna noodles, cooked, divided
2 cups grated mozzarella cheese, divided
1 cup Ricotta cheese, divided

†Marinated sun-dried tomatoes are available by the pound at most supermarkets. They have fuller flavor and are easier to use than dried tomatoes.

‡Use your favorite bottled or homemade marinara.

Place chopped artichoke hearts in a small bowl. Chop the sun-dried tomatoes and set aside. Do not cut too small. A rough cut is best so the tomatoes will be easier to spread when assembling the lasagna. In a small skillet, sauté onion in oil until translucent. Add the spinach to the onion and sauté until the spinach is wilted. Remove from skillet and set aside to cool. In the same pan, sauté the mushrooms until all the moisture is gone out of the pan and set mushrooms aside to cool.

Cover the bottom of a 9 x 13-inch baking dish with 1 cup marinara sauce. Cover with one layer of cooked lasagna noodles. Follow with 1 cup of marinara sauce. Sprinkle ½ cup artichoke hearts, ½ cup tomatoes, half of the spinach mixture, ½ cup mushrooms, ⅔ cup mozzarella cheese, and ½ cup Ricotta cheese. Repeat one more time, starting with the pasta. Finish with a final layer of pasta, ½ cup marinara, and the remaining ⅔ cup mozzarella cheese.

Bake in a 350-degree F. oven for twenty minutes or until cheese is golden and bubbly.

Lamb Curry with Fruited Rice

6–8 servings

For the lamb: In a 12-inch skillet, cook bacon until crispy. Crumble bacon and set aside. In the same skillet, brown the leg of lamb slices in oil and bacon drippings, partially cooking the slices. Once browned, remove meat from the skillet and set aside. In the same skillet, add onion, apple, celery, garlic, curry powder, salt, and cinnamon. Add water and return the meat to the pan. Cover and let simmer for 1 hour or until meat is tender. Skim off fat.

In a separate bowl, mix sour cream and cornstarch and gradually add ½ cup of the meat juices to the sour cream mixture. Once combined, add the sour cream mixture back into the skillet with the meat and sauce. Cook and stir until thickened and bubbly. When bubbly, continue to stir over heat for an additional 2 minutes and then transfer to a serving dish.

For the fruited rice: In a saucepan, combine water and salt and bring to a boil. Stir rice, apricots, and raisins into the boiling water. Cover and cook over low heat for 15 to 20 minutes or until rice is tender.

To serve, transfer lamb to a serving dish. Sprinkle bacon and chopped parsley over the top. Serve with fruited rice.

2 slices bacon
3 pounds boneless leg of lamb, cut into 1-inch slices
2 tablespoons canola oil
1 cup diced yellow onion
1 cup peeled and diced red apple
1 cup diced celery
1 clove garlic, minced
1 teaspoon curry powder
½ teaspoon salt
½ teaspoon cinnamon
1 cup water
1 cup sour cream
2 teaspoons cornstarch
2 teaspoons chopped parsley, for garnish

Fruited Rice

3 cups cold water
1 teaspoon salt
1¼ cups long grain rice
¼ cup dried apricots
¼ cup raisins

Pork Tenderloin Normandy with Dauphinoise Potatoes

6 servings

2 pounds pork tenderloin
1 tablespoon seasoning salt
½ cup unsalted butter, divided
3 cups water
1 lemon, juiced
2 medium Fuji apples, peeled and sliced
½ cup sugar
¾ cup balsamic vinegar
1 cup heavy whipping cream

Dauphinoise Potatoes

5 eggs
2 cups heavy cream
2 teaspoons salt
2 teaspoons garlic powder
6 large potatoes, peeled
2 cups shredded Asiago cheese

For the pork tenderloin: Clean silver skin and excess fat from pork tenderloin and thinly cover with seasoning salt. Sauté the pork in a large pan with ¼ cup butter. Remove from heat and transfer to a medium roasting pan. Place in a 350 degree F. oven for 20–25 minutes or until an internal temperature of 155 degrees F. is reached.

Combine water and lemon juice in a medium bowl. Add apple slices and set aside. Melt the remaining ¼ cup butter in a large sauté pan. Remove the apples from the water and sauté in the butter until golden. Add the sugar to the hot pan and sauté until the sugar has a caramel-like appearance. Remove apples with a slotted spoon and set aside to use as garnish.

To make the sauce, add balsamic vinegar to sugar and butter mixture in the pan and mix well. Cook on medium-high heat for about 3 minutes. Add cream and return to a boil and reduce until thickened.

For the potatoes: Combine eggs, cream, salt, and garlic powder until well mixed. Slice potatoes very thinly in a food processor and mix well with egg mixture. Spray a 9 x 13-inch baking dish with nonstick cooking spray. Spoon potatoes into pan and pat down. Pour egg mixture over potatoes and sprinkle Asiago cheese evenly over the top of the entire mixture. Bake at 325 degrees F. for 20 minutes and then rotate pan one-quarter turn and bake an additional 10 minutes. Increase the temperature to 375 degrees F. and bake for an additional 10–15 minutes or until the top of the dish is golden.

To serve, spoon heated sauce over the meat and place potatoes on the side. Garnish with caramelized apples.

4 servings

Pineapple-Glazed Pork Ribs

2 pounds baby back ribs
2 tablespoons sesame oil
¼ cup Chinese five-spice powder
Salt and pepper, to taste
1 tablespoon toasted sesame seeds, for garnish
Chopped cilantro, for garnish

Pineapple Glaze

2 tablespoons unsalted butter
1 pineapple, peeled and cubed
1 cup soy sauce
½ cup teriyaki sauce
¼ cup Hoisin sauce
¼ cup chili sauce
3 tablespoons rice wine vinegar
¼ cup brown sugar
1 red chili, thinly sliced
2 garlic cloves, minced
1 (2-inch) piece ginger, peeled and chopped

Preheat oven to 300 degrees F.

For the ribs: Arrange the ribs in a single layer in a shallow baking dish. Cover ribs with sesame oil and season generously with the spices. Roast for 2½ hours.

In the last 30 minutes of roasting time, baste the ribs with some of the glaze. When the ribs are done, the pork will pull away from the bone. Before serving, baste the ribs with more glaze and place them under the broiler for 6 minutes to give them a nice crust.

For the glaze: In a saucepan over medium heat, melt the butter and add the pineapple chunks; sauté for 3 minutes. Add remaining ingredients. Bring to a slow simmer and cook, stirring until thickened, about 20 minutes. Once it is thick, pour the glaze into a blender and purée until smooth.

To serve, sprinkle the pork ribs with sesame seeds and chopped cilantro.

6–8 servings

Apple-Stuffed Pork Loin

3 pounds pork loin
Salt and pepper, to taste

Sausage-Apple Stuffing

1 pound ground pork sausage
2½ cups peeled and finely chopped apples
2 cups ½-inch bread cubes
1 teaspoon ground cinnamon
¾ teaspoon salt
½ teaspoon allspice
1 cup apple juice

Chutney Sauce

1½ cups mayonnaise
1½ cups mango chutney†
1 teaspoon curry powder

†Mango chutney is available in most supermarkets.

For the pork loin: Cut pork loin into six to eight 6-ounce steak portions and then butterfly cut the portions so there is a pocket in the center of each steak. Season both sides with salt and pepper (see page 71 for instructions on how to butterfly cut).

Spoon ½-cup servings of stuffing into the pocket of each steak portion. Seal pockets with toothpicks.

Place stuffed pork loin steaks on a baking pan or in a shallow roasting pan. Roast in a 325 degree F. oven until meat thermometer registers an internal temperature of 155 degrees F., about 20–30 minutes.

For the stuffing: In a skillet, cook sausage until well done. Stir in apples, bread cubes, cinnamon, salt, and allspice. Add apple juice and toss to moisten.

For the sauce: Mix all ingredients together in a saucepan and warm over low heat.

To serve, spoon chutney sauce over baked pork loin steaks.

Fish and Chips

4 servings

Vegetable oil for deep frying
3 large russet potatoes
2½ cups flour, divided
1 tablespoon baking powder
3 teaspoons salt
½ teaspoon black pepper
1 (12-ounce) can soda water
1 large egg, lightly beaten
2 (8-ounce) cod fillets, cut in half on an angle
Salt, to taste

Heat oil in a deep, heavy skillet to 325 degrees F. To make the chips, peel the potatoes and cut them lengthwise into strips about the size of your index finger. Fry the chips for 3 minutes; they should not be fully cooked at this point. Remove the chips to a paper towel to drain. Increase the oil temperature to 375 degrees F.

In a large mixing bowl, combine 2 cups flour, baking powder, salt, and pepper. In a separate bowl combine the soda water and egg and pour into the flour mixture, whisking into a smooth batter. Spread the remaining ½ cup flour on a plate. Dredge each cod fillet in flour and then dip each into the batter, letting the excess drip off. Put the partially cooked chips in the bottom of the fryer basket and carefully submerge in the hot oil. Lower the battered fish into the oil on top of the chips. Fry the fish and chips for 5 minutes until crisp and brown. Remove the fish and chips onto paper towels; season lightly with salt.

Serve with malt vinegar and tartar sauce.

At one time, a jewelry store, a gift shop, an art gallery, and a men's clothing store were all located in the lobby of the Hotel Utah. The lobby is currently flanked on the west by the Nauvoo Café (where the old Union Pacific Railroad offices used to be) and on the east by the Bonneville Room. The restoration of the building in 1987 brought back the original design of 1911, with its woven carpets, marble floors, Scagliola-finished columns, and chandeliers. The Joseph Smith statue on the west side of the lobby is the size of Goliath, six cubits (nine feet five inches).

Rainbow Trout

6 servings

Combine cornmeal, flour, salt, and paprika in a shallow baking dish. Dredge fish in mixture. In a skillet, add a little oil and heat. When oil is hot, cook fish until lightly browned on one side.

After about 4 minutes, turn fish and brown other side about 4 minutes. Cook until fish flakes easily when tested with fork. Further enhance the flavor of the crispy, cornmeal-coated trout with a squeeze of fresh lemon juice.

⅔ cup yellow cornmeal
¼ cup all-purpose flour
2 teaspoons salt
½ teaspoon paprika
6 large fresh trout
Canola oil
Juice from fresh lemon

Alaskan Salmon Burgers

4 servings

For the burgers: Preheat oven to 400 degrees F. In a medium bowl, combine parsley, eggs, onion, bread crumbs, salt, pepper, lemon zest, and dill mayonnaise. Add salmon and mix together well. Make 4 patties and set aside. Heat a large skillet on medium; add 2 tablespoons of oil. Place burgers in skillet. Cook over medium heat until browned. Turn and brown other side. Place in oven for 4 minutes.

For the mayonnaise: Mix all ingredients in a small bowl.

Serve salmon burgers topped with Dill Mayonnaise on toasted buns.

2 teaspoons freshly chopped parsley
2 eggs
¼ cup finely diced onion
½ cup finely ground bread crumbs
1 teaspoon salt
½ teaspoon black pepper
Zest of 1 lemon
¼ cup Dill Mayonnaise (recipe below)
2 (6.5-ounce) cans Alaska skinless and boneless salmon, drained well
2 tablespoons olive oil

Dill Mayonnaise

½ cup mayonnaise
½ lemon, juiced
2 tablespoons freshly chopped dill leaves
Cayenne pepper, to taste
½ teaspoon salt
½ teaspoon pepper

SHRIMP SCAMPI

4 servings

1½ pounds cooked jumbo shrimp, shelled and deveined
Salt and fresh ground pepper, to taste
4 tablespoons unsalted butter, divided
2 teaspoons minced garlic
1 tablespoon freshly squeezed lemon juice
¼ teaspoon grated lemon zest
2 teaspoons finely chopped flat-leaf parsley leaves
4 ¼-inch lime slices
8–12 cherry tomatoes

Linguine

1 tablespoon canola oil
1 teaspoon salt
8 cups water
1 (16-ounce) package linguine

For the shrimp: Put the shrimp on a large plate and pat dry with a paper towel. Arrange the shrimp so they lie flat and are evenly spaced.

Heat a large skillet over medium heat. Season the shrimp with salt and pepper. Add 2 tablespoons butter and the garlic to the skillet. Raise the heat to high and add the shrimp. Cook the shrimp for about 1 minute. Spoon the shrimp into a bowl.

Return the skillet to the heat and add the lemon juice and remaining 2 tablespoons butter to create a sauce. Stir in the lemon zest and parsley. Pour the sauce over the shrimp. Add cooked linguine and season with salt and pepper.

For the linguine: Add 1 tablespoon canola oil and 1 teaspoon salt to 8 cups of water in a stockpot. When water comes to a boil, add the linguine and cook 6–8 minutes.

To serve, make a bed of pasta in a pasta bowl and cover with the shrimp scampi. Garnish with cherry tomatoes and lime slices.

Baked Pacific Salmon with Pineapple Raspberry Salsa

8 servings

8 (6-ounce) salmon fillets
Salt and pepper, to taste
4 tablespoons olive oil, divided

Pineapple Raspberry Salsa

½ medium red onion, diced
½ green bell pepper, seeded and diced
½ yellow bell pepper, seeded and diced
½ red bell pepper, seeded and diced
½ jalapeño pepper, seeded and diced
½ ripe pineapple, cored and diced
1 bunch cilantro, stems removed and finely chopped
⅓ cup extra-virgin olive oil
¼ cup rice wine vinegar
3 tablespoons granulated sugar
2 teaspoons crushed red peppers
Salt, to taste
1 (6-ounce) package fresh raspberries

For the salmon: Season the salmon fillets with salt and pepper and sauté 4 at a time in 2 tablespoons olive oil until lightly browned. Transfer to a baking sheet that has been lightly sprayed with nonstick cooking spray. Bake in a 350 degree F. oven until the salmon is flaky, approximately 10–12 minutes.

For the salsa: Combine onion, peppers, pineapple, and cilantro in a small bowl and toss together.

In a separate bowl, mix oil and vinegar with the sugar and set aside until the sugar has dissolved and then add the crushed red pepper. Pour the vinaigrette onto the vegetable mixture and toss until everything is well coated. Adjust the flavor with salt. Just before serving, lightly toss the raspberries with the salsa.

To serve, put the baked salmon on a lightly heated plate and spoon several spoonfuls of the Pineapple Raspberry Salsa onto the fish, making sure to get some of the juice from the salsa as well. This dish is best served with oven-roasted potatoes and steamed asparagus.

Poached Salmon

6–8 servings

For the salmon: In a large shallow pan, heat the water on the stovetop. When the water is just below the boiling point, add thyme, lemon, and salmon. Cook salmon in pan until it is cooked all the way through and appears to flake, about 8–14 minutes depending on the size. Transfer to a serving dish or platter.

For sauce: Combine all ingredients together and heat slowly over low heat until warm.

To serve, spoon Hollandaise sauce over salmon.

3 pounds fresh salmon cut into 6-ounce portions
1 gallon water
1 teaspoon chopped fresh thyme
1 lemon, cut into wedges

Hollandaise Sauce

1 cup sour cream
1 cup mayonnaise
¼ cup lemon juice
½ teaspoon Tabasco sauce

Located on the northeast corner of Main Street and South Temple, the Hotel Utah had easy access to streetcars and the railway. It was built on land once occupied by the general tithing office of The Church of Jesus Christ of Latter-day Saints, the old Adobe Mint, a bishop's storehouse, and the Deseret News printing plant. In 2000, the Church converted the section of Main Street between North and South Temple into Temple Square Plaza, with awe-inspiring water features and flower beds. The west side of the Joseph Smith Memorial Building now opens onto the plaza.

Pistachio and Pine Nut–Crusted Salmon

4 servings

Roasted pistachios and pine nuts

¼ cup pine nuts
¼ cup pistachios

Salmon

4 (6-ounce) salmon fillets
¼ cup Dijon mustard
1 cup bread crumbs
2 tablespoons dried parsley
2 tablespoons dried thyme
1 tablespoon granulated garlic
¼ cup butter

For roasted pistachios and pine nuts: Spread nuts evenly on a baking sheet and place in 350 degree F. oven for 10–15 minutes or until golden.

For the salmon: Brush each salmon fillet with Dijon mustard. Place pine nuts, pistachios, bread crumbs, parsley, thyme, and garlic into a food processor and chop until fine. Be careful not to overprocess the mixture, as it will become pasty. Add the butter and pulse 5 or 6 times until all the butter is incorporated. Place 2–3 tablespoons of the crumb mixture onto each fillet and spread evenly over the salmon, pressing the mixture firmly into the fillet. Bake in a 350 degree F. oven for 12–15 minutes.

Serve with oven-roasted new red potatoes and a tangy peach salsa.

Jambalaya

6–8 servings

¼ cup diced bacon (3–4 strips)
¼ cup diced yellow onion
1 teaspoon chopped garlic
¼ cup diced celery
¼ cup diced green peppers
3 cups diced tomatoes
½ cup tomato purée
1 cup water
½ teaspoon thyme
1 teaspoon salt
1 teaspoon Old Bay Seasoning
1 cup diced cooked Italian sausage
1 cup diced cooked chicken
1 pound cooked shrimp (approximately 40–50), tails off
3 cups cooked rice
2 sprigs parsley, for garnish
3 green onions, chopped, for garnish

Fry bacon, drain, and set aside. Sauté the onion, garlic, celery, and peppers in the bacon fat. Add tomatoes, tomato purée, water, thyme, salt, and Old Bay Seasoning. Simmer for 10–15 minutes. Add meats, shrimp, and rice and simmer for 10 minutes. Add more water if necessary.

To serve, garnish with parsley or green onion.

6 servings

Stuffed Portobello Mushrooms

¼ cup diced red onion
1 clove garlic, minced
¼ cup unsalted butter
½ cup diced yellow squash
½ cup diced zucchini
½ cup diced eggplant
¼ cup diced Roma tomatoes
¼ cup tomato purée
Salt and pepper, to taste
6 large Portobello mushrooms
2 tablespoons olive oil
¼ cup grated Asiago cheese†

†If Asiago cheese is not available, grated Parmesan may be substituted.

Sauté onion and garlic in the butter until the onion begins to brown. Add the squash, zucchini, and eggplant and sauté until the squash is tender, but do not let it cook too long. Add the Roma tomatoes and the tomato purée. Adjust the flavor with salt and pepper. Remove from the heat and set aside.

Remove the stem and ribs from the Portobello mushrooms and lightly brush with olive oil. Spoon about ½ cup of the squash mixture into each mushroom and sprinkle with Asiago cheese. Bake in a 350-degree F. oven for 12–15 minutes or until the cheese becomes golden brown.

This dish is best served with a zesty marinara sauce.

WHITE CHOCOLATE MOUSSE OREO CAKE (PAGE 115)

Desserts

5 servings

Lemon Meringue Pie Parfaits

Lemon Curd

4 large eggs
1 cup sugar
⅔ cup freshly squeezed lemon juice
Zest of 1 lemon, freshly grated
¼ cup cold unsalted butter, cut into pieces

Meringue Kisses

3 egg whites
¾ cup sugar
¼ teaspoon cream of tartar
1 teaspoon vanilla

1 (12-ounce) box Nilla Wafers or other butter cookies
Whipped cream, slightly sweetened
Crispy meringue kisses (store-bought are fine)
Lemon slices, for garnish

For the lemon curd: Make lemon curd the day before you plan to serve the dessert. Bring about an inch of water to a simmer in a large saucepan. In a mixing bowl that will fit inside the saucepan (don't place in saucepan yet), whisk the eggs and sugar together until very light yellow and fluffy. Use a mixer fitted with a whisk attachment, if possible. Whisk in lemon juice and lemon zest. Place the mixing bowl in the saucepan, with the bowl's base above the simmering water (pour out some of the water if necessary). Cook, whisking occasionally, until the mixture is thickened and custardy, about 15 minutes. Remove bowl from the heat and stir in butter. Let cool, cover, and refrigerate overnight. You can also use a double boiler to make the curd.

For the meringue kisses: Beat egg whites in a small mixing bowl until stiff fluffy white peaks form. Slowly add sugar, cream of tartar, and vanilla and continue to mix. Fill a pastry bag or large zipper-top bag with the mixture and pipe small drops onto parchment paper on a cookie sheet. Bake at 200 degrees F. for 3 hours. Kisses will have a light, hollow feel to them. If they are still sticky, bake a few minutes longer.

To assemble, crumble a few cookies in the bottom of a clear glass and then spoon in a layer of lemon curd. Follow with a layer of whipped cream and then a few meringue kisses. Repeat the layers, ending with the kisses. Garnish with cookie wedges and a lemon slice.

10–14 servings

Pecan Tart

Crust

½ cup butter, softened
½ cup granulated sugar
1 egg
1 egg yolk
½ teaspoon almond extract
1 tablespoon heavy whipping cream
2 cups all-purpose flour
1 cup whole pecan nuts

Filling

½ cup granulated sugar
1 egg
½ cup corn syrup
1 tablespoon melted butter
1 teaspoon vanilla

For the crust: In mixing bowl, combine butter and sugar and then add egg, egg yolk, almond extract, and cream. Mix together and beat until smooth. Add flour and mix well. Roll dough and put into well-greased, 9-inch fluted tart pan. Put pecan nuts on top of prepared dough. Pour filling over nuts.

For the filling: In a bowl, combine all ingredients and mix with a spoon until sugar dissolves.

Bake at 350 degrees F. for 45–50 minutes.

Serving amount varies depending on slice sizes. If desired, garnish with a dollop of whipped cream.

When the hotel opened its doors in 1911, a hotel suite cost anywhere from one dollar and fifty cents to six dollars. Three Presidents of the LDS Church actually resided in the hotel: Presidents David O. McKay, Spencer W. Kimball, and Ezra Taft Benson. The building was decommissioned as a hotel in 1987, and was reopened in 1993 as the Joseph Smith Memorial Building by its owner, The Church of Jesus Christ of Latter-day Saints, which had converted the building to offices, banquet halls, and community meeting halls.

Key Lime Pie

8 servings

For the pie filling: Beat egg yolks in medium bowl on low speed of electric mixer. Gradually beat in sweetened condensed milk and lime juice until smooth. Blend in cream, lime zest, and food coloring, if desired. Pour into pie crust. Bake at 350 degrees F. for 25 minutes. Remove from oven.

For the whipped cream: In a mixing bowl, whip cream, sugar, and vanilla until soft peaks form and hold their shape.

To serve, top pie with whipped cream and sprinkle with toasted coconut flakes.

4 egg yolks
1 (14-ounce) can sweetened condensed milk
½ cup fresh lime juice
¾ cup heavy cream
1 teaspoon lime zest
2 or 3 drops green food coloring, optional
1 (9-inch) graham cracker pie crust
½ cup toasted coconut flakes, for garnish

Whipped Cream

2 cups heavy cream
½ cup powdered sugar
1 teaspoon vanilla

Key Lime Tartlets

9 servings (2 each)

Make Key Lime Pie filling. Place tart shells on baking sheet and divide filling evenly among the shells. Bake at 350 degrees F. for 18–20 minutes. Let cool for 30 minutes.

To serve, top with a dollop of whipped cream piped through a pastry bag.

1 recipe Key Lime Pie filling (above)
18 (2-inch) tart shells
½ recipe Whipped Cream (above)

8 servings

Fruit Tart

Crust

½ cup butter, softened
½ cup granulated sugar
1 egg
1 egg yolk
½ teaspoon vanilla extract
1 tablespoon heavy cream
2 cups all-purpose flour
¼ cup melted semisweet chocolate chips
Kiwis, blueberries, strawberries, mandarin oranges, or your favorite fruit or berries

Pastry Cream

½ cup granulated sugar
1 tablespoon cornstarch
1 cup whole milk
2 egg yolks, beaten
1 tablespoon butter
½ teaspoon vanilla extract

For the crust: In a mixing bowl, combine butter and sugar and then add egg, egg yolk, vanilla extract, and cream. Mix together and beat until smooth. Add flour and mix well. Roll dough and put into well-greased, 9-inch fluted pan. Bake at 350 degrees F. for 15–17 minutes. Remove to wire rack and cool. Brush bottom of tart crust with melted chocolate and let it cool.

For the pastry cream: Mix sugar, cornstarch, and milk together in a heavy saucepan over medium-high heat until sugar is dissolved, stirring continually, and then bring to boil. Cook about 2 minutes until thick and clear. To prevent cooking the eggs, mix the egg yolks with a small amount of hot mixture first, and then combine both mixtures together. Bring again to a boil, stirring continually. Remove from heat; add butter and vanilla and let it cool.

Spread pastry cream on top of brushed chocolate inside tart crust.

To serve, decorate top of tart with any desired amount of your favorite fruit or berries.

Chocolate-Dipped Strawberries

6–8 servings

- 2 pints fresh strawberries
- 1 pound semisweet chocolate
- 1 pound white chocolate

Wash strawberries with cold water and towel dry. Melt chocolate in the microwave in a microwave-safe bowl for 30 seconds. Remove bowl and stir the chocolate. Repeat the 30-seconds-and-stir rotation until the chocolate is smooth and runny. Be careful not to burn the chocolate. Line a baking sheet with parchment paper. Dip the strawberries in the melted chocolate and place them on the parchment paper to let the chocolate set up.

For an added flair, melt a small amount of white chocolate and drizzle it over the already covered berries.

Choux Paste (Éclair)

10–12 servings

- 1 cup water
- ½ cup butter
- 1 cup all-purpose flour
- 1 pinch salt
- 5 eggs
- 1 recipe Pastry Cream (page 118)
- 1 recipe Ganache (page 110), optional

Heat water and butter in large saucepan until butter is melted; bring to a boil. Add flour and salt; continue to stir. Mixture should form a smooth paste that leaves the side of the pan clean. Put hot paste mixture into electric mixer and beat with paddle attachment, adding eggs one at a time. Beat in each addition until paste is smooth and glossy. Line baking sheet with parchment paper. Put paste in pastry bag with a star tip and pipe out 3-inch-long strips of dough spaced 2–3 inches apart. Bake at 400 degrees F. for 35–40 minutes. Cool to room temperature, about 15–20 minutes.

To assemble, make a small ½-inch slit on top of each pastry shell. Using a pastry bag with a round tip, fill the crust with pastry cream. Frost tops with your favorite chocolate frosting or dip in chocolate Ganache (page 110).

Carrot Cake

12–15 servings

2 cups sugar
1 cup canola oil
4 eggs
2 cups all-purpose flour
1 teaspoon salt
1 teaspoon baking soda
2 teaspoons ground cinnamon
½ cup golden raisins
3 cups shredded raw carrots

Cream Cheese Icing

1 pound cream cheese, softened
½ cup butter, softened
5 cups powdered sugar
2 teaspoons vanilla

For the cake: In a large bowl, combine sugar, oil, and eggs and mix until creamy. Add flour, salt, baking soda, and cinnamon and mix well. Stir in raisins and carrots and beat until well blended. Pour batter into a 9 x 13-inch greased baking dish and bake at 350 degrees F. for 45–50 minutes. Place on cooling rack. When completely cool, frost with cream cheese icing.

For the icing: Beat cream cheese and butter until blended. Add powdered sugar and vanilla; beat until smooth and fluffy.

Cheesecake

12–16 servings

Filling

3 (8-ounce) packages cream cheese (room temperature)
1 cup granulated sugar
½ cup sour cream
6 eggs
1 teaspoon vanilla
½ teaspoon salt
1 tablespoon orange zest, optional
Whipped cream, for garnish
Fresh fruit, for garnish

Graham Cracker Crust

8 ounces graham crackers, crushed (about 2 sleeves)
¼ cup melted butter
¼ cup sugar

For the filling: Blend cream cheese and sugar in a 5-quart mixer with a paddle attachment. Scrape down the bowl several times during mixing. Add sour cream, eggs, and remaining ingredients and blend until smooth.

For the crust: Blend ingredients using a hand whisk. Press mixture evenly into the bottom of a 9-inch springform pan.

Pour cream cheese mixture over the crust and bake at 350 degrees F. for 1 hour. It is important to place another baking dish with 1 inch of water in it on the rack below the cheesecake to create a moist baking environment.

To serve, garnish with whipped cream and fresh fruit.

During World War II, the Hotel Utah supported the war effort by printing a daily bulletin entitled "Today's War News" for its patrons and customers. The hotel advertised that "Quality and service will never be rationed at Hotel Utah," but a warning to patrons said, "Don't order more than you can eat and then eat all you order." Pictured is the enclosed portion of the Roof Gardens that faced the Utah State Capitol Building in 1911.

Chocolate Mint Cake

12–16 servings

- 1 package devil's food cake mix
- ½ recipe White Chocolate Mousse (page 114)
- ½ recipe Dark Chocolate Mousse (page 114)
- 2 tablespoons mint extract
- 2–3 drops green food coloring
- 1 recipe Ganache (below)
- Chocolate mint truffles, for garnish
- Apple slices or berries, for garnish

Prepare cake mix according to package directions. For a 3-layer cake, divide batter among three 9-inch round pans and bake as directed. Set aside to cool. For 4 layers, bake two 9-inch rounds, cool, and then cut each in half horizontally.

Prepare half of White Chocolate Mousse recipe (page 114). Add mint extract and green food coloring. Alternate cake layers with mint mousse in between each one. Cover the top and around the edges with the Dark Chocolate Mousse. Place in the refrigerator to set.

Prepare Ganache and pour evenly over the top of the Dark Chocolate Mousse. Garnish with chocolate mint truffles, apple slices, or berries.

Ganache

Makes about 3½ cups

- 2 cups heavy cream
- 2½ (8-ounce) semisweet chocolate baking bars

Scald cream in a small saucepan. Chop chocolate into pieces. Remove cream from heat and add chocolate. Stir until chocolate is completely melted. As the mixture cools it will thicken and be easier to spread as the topping on éclairs or cakes.

Ganache can be stored at room temperature for 7 days or in the refrigerator up to 1 month. If storing in the refrigerator, place a sheet of plastic wrap directly on top of ganache in bowl so it doesn't dry out. It also works well as a chocolate spread for crêpes or waffles. Ganache can be reheated in a double boiler.

12–14 servings

White Raspberry Cake

1 package white cake mix
1 (16-ounce) can raspberry filling
1 cup fresh raspberries, for garnish

Whipped Cream Frosting

2 cups heavy cream
½ cup powdered sugar
1 teaspoon vanilla

Raspberry Sauce

½ cup raspberry jam
1 tablespoon warm water

For the cake: Prepare and bake cake following the package directions for two 9-inch round cakes. Cool and cut each cake layer into two layers so that you have four layers. Spread raspberry filling evenly between the four layers and chill for 30 minutes.

For the frosting: In a mixing bowl, whip cream, sugar, and vanilla until soft peaks form and hold their shape.

For the sauce: Combine raspberry jam with warm water and mix well.

Frost the sides of the cake with frosting. Drizzle sauce over top and garnish with fresh raspberries.

12–14 servings

Red Velvet Cake

1 package red velvet cake mix
1 chocolate bar, semisweet or dark chocolate, for garnish

Cream Cheese Icing

2 (8-ounce) packages cream cheese, softened
½ cup butter, at room temperature
5 cups powdered sugar
2 teaspoons vanilla

For the cake: Prepare cake as directed on the package for two 9-inch round cakes. Cool and cut each layer into two layers so you have four layers.

For the icing: Beat cream cheese until creamy. Add butter and mix until blended. Add powdered sugar and beat on low until blended. Add vanilla and beat on medium speed until smooth and fluffy.

Frost each cake layer with cream cheese icing as you stack them upon each other and then frost the top and sides.

Shave chocolate bar with potato peeler or cheese grater. Top cake with shaved chocolate bar.

Dark Chocolate Mousse

Serves 10

14 ounces dark chocolate
7 egg yolks
½ cup honey or corn syrup
2 cups heavy cream
Fresh berries, for garnish
Whipped cream, for garnish

Chop chocolate into chunks and carefully melt in a double boiler or in the microwave. In a separate bowl, whip yolks to soft peaks. In a small saucepan, bring honey to a boil. While the honey is still hot, pour it into the yolks, stirring constantly, and whip until thick. Fold warm chocolate into yolk mixture. In a medium bowl, whip cream to soft peaks and fold into chocolate mixture.

Separate into individual serving dishes, such as chilled glasses. For a more elegant look, pipe the mousse into the dish or spoon with an ice cream scoop. Chill 2 hours before serving.

To serve, garnish with fresh berries and whipped cream, if desired.

White Chocolate Mousse

Serves 10

1 pouch unflavored Knox gelatin
4 ounces white chocolate
2 egg yolks
1 tablespoon honey or corn syrup
2 tablespoons milk
3 cups heavy cream
Berries, for garnish
Mint leaves, for garnish

Prepare powdered gelatin according to package instructions. Let set. Once set, place pan in cold water to soften gelatin enough to loosen it from the pan. Place softened gelatin into a double boiler and melt.

In a separate double boiler, melt the chocolate, being careful not to burn it. Add melted chocolate to gelatin and mix well.

Whip egg yolks by hand in a small bowl to soft foamy peaks. Meanwhile, bring honey to a boil. Pour hot honey onto the yolks, stirring constantly. Fold the melted chocolate into the yolk mixture. Heat the milk in a small saucepan. Stir the milk into the chocolate mixture.

In a large bowl, whip the cream to soft peaks and fold into the chocolate mixture.

Pour into prepared dishes and chill at least 2 hours before serving. To serve, garnish with a fresh berry and mint leaf.

White Chocolate Mousse Oreo Cake *(photo page 98)*

(photo page 98)

12–16 servings

Crust

2½ cups crushed Oreo cookie crumbs

½ cup butter, melted

Filling

1 recipe White Chocolate Mousse (page 114)

Whipped Cream

1 cup heavy cream

1 tablespoon powdered sugar

½ teaspoon vanilla

Fresh berries, kiwis, or oranges, for garnish

For the crust and filling: Mix Oreo cookie crumbs with butter. Press evenly onto the bottom and sides of an 8-inch springform pan and set in freezer while filling is being made. Pour white chocolate mousse into crust. Freeze again for 4 hours or overnight. After freezing, carefully remove sides of springform pan and slide cake onto a platter.

For whipped cream: Pour cream into a bowl and start mixing with a hand mixer. Gradually add sugar and vanilla while mixing. Beat until soft peaks form.

To serve, top cake with dollops of whipped cream and garnish with desired fruits.

In 1914, the Roof Gardens of the Hotel Utah lay claim to being second to none in the country. In 1960, the management revamped the Starlite Gardens and moved the restaurant to the west wing only. A "name the restaurant" contest brought in 1,200 entries. The winner was promised a table for four once a month for twelve months. From then until 1976, the restaurant was known as Hotel Utah Sky Room.

Crème Brûlée

10 servings

3 cups heavy cream
6 egg yolks
1 cup sugar, divided
1 teaspoon vanilla
Fresh berries, for garnish

Preheat oven to 300 degrees F. In a sturdy medium saucepan, heat cream until it just comes to a boil. Meanwhile, in a medium bowl, whisk egg yolks, ¼ cup sugar, and vanilla until combined. Gradually whisk warm cream into egg yolk mixture.

In a small saucepan, melt and burn ½ cup sugar until it is a light caramel color. Gradually whisk sugar into the cream and egg mixture until well blended.

Place ten 2-ounce ramekins in a 9 x 13-inch baking pan. Divide cream mixture evenly among the ramekins. Place baking pan into oven and pour hot water into baking pan until it is about ¼-inch deep.

Bake for 35–40 minutes (until the centers appear set when gently shaken). Remove ramekins from water, cool, and chill.

To serve, sprinkle the extra ¼ cup sugar evenly over the top of the custards. Burn the sugar using a blow torch until caramel brown. Garnish with fresh berries.

Flan

6–8 servings

1 cup sugar, divided
2 cups whole milk
1 large egg
½ teaspoon vanilla extract

For the caramel, burn ½ cup sugar in a small saucepan over high heat until it is a light brown liquid. Pour caramel sugar into a 9-inch cake pan and spread evenly from side to side.

In a medium bowl, mix milk, egg, ½ cup sugar, and vanilla with wire whisk. Pour into the cake pan over the caramel. Bake at 300 degrees F. for 55 minutes with a pan of water on a lower oven rack to create steam. Remove from oven to cool.

To serve, slide knife around the edge to free flan from cake pan. Flip flan onto dish; the caramel sauce will be on top of the flan. Serve chilled.

Chocolate Custard

10 servings

- 1½ cups heavy cream
- 1½ cups whole milk
- ¾ cup semisweet chocolate chips
- 3 egg yolks
- 2 eggs
- ¼ cup sugar
- Raspberries, for garnish
- Mint leaves, for garnish

In a medium saucepan, heat cream and milk until it just comes to a boil. Stir in chocolate chips and remove from heat. Meanwhile, in a medium bowl, whisk egg yolks, eggs, and sugar until combined. Gradually whisk warm chocolate cream into egg mixture until well blended.

Pour into ten 2-ounce ramekins. Bake at 300 degrees F. for 35–40 minutes with a pan of hot water on the rack below to create steam.

To serve, garnish with raspberries and a mint leaf.

Pastry Cream

Makes about 3 cups

- ¾ cup sugar
- 2½ tablespoons cornstarch
- ⅛ teaspoon salt
- 2 cups milk
- 3 egg yolks, beaten
- 2 tablespoons butter
- 1 teaspoon vanilla

Mix sugar, cornstarch, salt, and milk together in a heavy saucepan until dissolved, stirring constantly while bringing to a boil. Cook about 2 minutes until thick and clear. To prevent cooking the eggs, mix the egg yolks with a small amount of the hot mixture first, and then incorporate all together. Bring mixture again to a boil, stirring constantly, and then remove from the heat. Add the butter and vanilla. Cover with plastic wrap, making sure the plastic touches the surface to prevent a film from forming. Refrigerate.

This pastry cream may be used as pie or eclair filling as well. Add bananas, coconut, or cocoa, to taste, for your favorite pie.

DECADENCE

8–10 servings

For the decadence: Spray one 9-inch cake pan with nonstick cooking spray. Finely chop both chocolates. Bring water and ¾ cup sugar to a boil. Remove from heat and stir in chocolate until completely melted. Stir butter into chocolate mixture.

Whip eggs with ⅓ cup sugar to form soft foamy peaks. Fold egg mixture into chocolate mixture. Pour into cake pan and bake at 350 degrees F. for about 40 minutes. It is important to place another baking dish with an inch of water in it on the rack below the Decadence to create a moist baking environment. Chill at least 2 hours before unmolding.

For the topping: In a mixing bowl, whip cream, sugar, and vanilla, until soft peaks form and hold their shape.

To serve, spread the topping over the entire chocolate Decadence. Add dollops of topping around the edge as a garnish. Sprinkle cocoa powder over the top.

6 ounces semisweet baking chocolate (comes in 8-ounce bar)
7 ounces unsweetened baking chocolate (comes in 8-ounce bar)
½ cup water
¾ cup granulated sugar
1 cup soft butter
6 eggs
⅓ cup granulated sugar
1 teaspoon cocoa powder

Whipped Cream Topping

2 cups heavy cream
½ cup powdered sugar
1 teaspoon vanilla

In 1936, the cost for dinner and dancing in the Empire Room was just two dollars and fifty cents a person. Will Rogers was once denied entrance to the Empire Room as he lacked a coat and tie. After borrowing the needed items from the front desk, he returned to the room and was granted admittance. The paintings that encircle the room were originally painted on burlap and then shellacked. They fell apart when they were taken down to be cleaned. New paintings were commissioned and re-created by artist Judith Mehr.

Makes 20–24 cookies

Coconut Macaroons

- 2 cups coconut
- 2¼ cups granulated sugar
- 1 cup flour
- Pinch of salt
- 1½ tablespoons corn syrup
- ¾ cup hot water
- 2 large eggs
- 1 teaspoon vanilla
- 1 cup milk chocolate chips, melted

Mix coconut, sugar, flour, and salt in a mixing bowl. In a separate bowl, add corn syrup to water and dissolve. Add eggs and vanilla. With a mixer on low speed, add liquid ingredients to dry ingredients and mix until evenly blended. Allow mixture to rest and absorb moisture for 30 minutes. Scoop onto cookie sheet with an ice cream scoop. Bake at 350 degrees F. for 18–20 minutes.

For added flair, dip half of the cookie in melted chocolate chips and place on wax paper to set up.

16 servings

Brioche

- 1 tablespoon dried yeast
- 3 tablespoons sugar
- 4¼ cups flour, divided
- 1 teaspoon salt
- 4 eggs, lightly beaten
- ½ cup warm milk
- ¾ cup butter, softened

Filling

- 1 recipe Pastry Cream (page 118)

Glaze

- ½ cup jam (any flavor)
- 2 tablespoons warm water
- Fresh berries, for garnish

For the dough: In a mixing bowl, combine yeast, sugar, 4 cups flour, and salt. Add beaten eggs. Start mixer on low speed and slowly add milk, beating until it is well combined. Gradually incorporate softened butter into the dough. Switch speed to medium and mix 5 minutes. Dough will be very sticky. Sprinkle working surface, hands, and dough with a small amount of the extra ¼ cup flour. Knead dough until smooth and elastic. Divide into 2 pieces and let rest for 20 minutes. With a rolling pin, roll the dough and place in two 9 or 10-inch foil tins or pie dishes.

For the filling: Prepare Pastry Cream. Fill each shell with half of the pastry cream. Cover with plastic wrap and let rise for 20–30 minutes. Bake at 350 degrees F. for 25 minutes or until golden and cooked. Cool after baking.

For the glaze: Add water to jam in tiny increments until it is thin enough to brush on.

To serve, top brioche with your favorite berries or mixed berries and cover with the glaze.

VEGETARIAN LASAGNA (PAGE 80)

Illustration and Caption Credits

Food Photos

By Robert Casey: pages 2, 5, 9, 10, 15, 20, 23, 25, 28, 33, 34, 38, 41, 43, 46, 49, 53, 56, 59, 60, 63, 67, 70, 73, 77, 82, 85, 88, 91, 95, 97, 98, 101, 105, 106, 110, 113, 116, 121, 122, front and back covers

By John Luke: pages 18 and 55

Food styling of all food photos by Maxine Bramwell

Historical Photos

Pages vi, 13, 17, 27, 31, 37, 75, 78, 93, 115. Used by permission, Utah State Historical Society.

Pages viii, 44, 45, 51, 64, 87, 102, 109, 119. Used by permission, Temple Square Hospitality Corporation.

Caption Information

The captions are a compilation of information from the following sources:

- Leonard J. Arrington and Heidi Swinton, *The Hotel Utah, Salt Lake's Classy Lady* (Salt Lake City: Publisher Press, 1986).
- Joseph Bauman, "The Old Hotel Utah Has Long, Storied History of Salt Lake," *Deseret News,* March 16, 2009.
- "Joseph Smith Memorial Building," http://en.wikipedia.org/wiki/Joseph_Smith_Memorial_Building (accessed Nov. 4, 2010).
- The Joseph Smith Memorial Building tour guide instruction booklet.

Metric Conversions

Volume Conversions		
1 milliliter	=	slightly less than ¼ teaspoon
2 milliliters	=	slightly less than ½ teaspoon
5 milliliters	=	1 teaspoon
15 milliliters	=	1 tablespoon
59 milliliters	=	¼ cup
79 milliliters	=	⅓ cup
237 milliliters	=	1 cup
0.946 liter	=	4 cups = 1 quart
1 liter	=	1.06 quarts
3.8 liters	=	4 quarts = 1 gallon

Weight Conversions		
28 grams	=	1 ounce
113 grams	=	4 ounces
227 grams	=	8 ounces
454 grams	=	16 ounces = 1 pound

Equivalent Measurements

3 teaspoons	=	1 tablespoon
4 tablespoons	=	¼ cup
5 tablespoons + 1 teaspoon	=	⅓ cup
8 tablespoons	=	½ cup
10 tablespoons + 2 teaspoons	=	⅔ cup
12 tablespoons	=	¾ cup
16 tablespoons	=	1 cup = 8 fluid ounces
2 cups	=	1 pint = 16 fluid ounces
4 cups	=	2 pints = 1 quart = 32 fluid ounces
2 quarts	=	½ gallon = 64 fluid ounces
4 quarts	=	1 gallon = 128 fluid ounces

Emergency Substitutions

Recipe results will vary when using substitutes. Use only in emergency circumstances.

Missing	Amount	Replace with
Powdered sugar	1 cup	1 cup granulated sugar + 1 teaspoon cornstarch, mixed in blender
Unsweetened chocolate	1 ounce	3 tablespoons cocoa powder + 1 tablespoon vegetable oil OR 1½ ounces bittersweet chocolate (remove 1 tablespoon sugar from recipe)
Bittersweet chocolate	1 ounce	4 tablespoons cocoa powder + 2 tablespoons butter OR ⅔ ounce unsweetened chocolate + 2 teaspoons sugar
Milk	1 cup	½ cup evaporated milk + ½ cup water OR ¼ cup nonfat dry milk + ⅞ cup water + 2 teaspoons butter
Buttermilk	1 cup	1 cup milk + 1 tablespoon lemon juice (stir together and let sit 5 minutes before use)
Whole milk	1 cup	⅝ cup skim milk + ⅜ cup half and half OR ⅔ cup 1% milk + ⅓ cup half and half OR ¾ cup 2% milk + ¼ cup half and half
Half-and-half	1 cup	¾ cup whole milk + ¼ cup heavy cream OR ⅔ cup skim or lowfat milk + ⅓ cup heavy cream
Cornstarch (for thickening)	1 Tbsp	2 tablespoons flour
Flour (for thickening)	1 Tbsp	½ to ⅔ tablespoon cornstarch
Cake flour	1 cup	⅞ cup all-purpose flour + 2 tablespoons cornstarch
Self-rising flour	1 cup	1 cup all-purpose flour + 1½ teaspoons baking powder + ½ teaspoon salt
Baking powder	1 tsp	¼ teaspoon baking soda + ½ teaspoon cream of tartar

Index

T

V

W